This little book is a valuable reprint of a collection of seven sermons by Robert Murray McCheyne. The book's title is an abbreviation of the second sermon, 'The Believer's Joy in God.' The style of preaching, common in the first half of the nineteenth century, is mostly a mixture of textual and topical exposition. What makes the work valuable, however, and well worth reading today, is the way in which McCheyne drives home the glory, the blessedness, the sheer joy of truly knowing God in Christ, of delighting in his ways, his Word, his holiness. Here is no self-absorbed emphasis on contemporary human flourishing, but life lived with one foot in eternity.

**D. A. CARSON**
Research Professor of New Testament,
Trinity Evangelical Divinity School, Deerfield, Illinois

Warning dear reader, you are about to be ushered into the place of true Christian joy by one who understood. You may never have experienced Christian joy, or you may have experienced joy at a time in your life and then lost it. Be encouraged, Robert Murray McCheyne will take you right to the source. In his clear and compelling way, McCheyne weeds out all the false paths to joy, even many Christian ones, and invites you to the Well Himself, Jesus Christ. This book is a must read, and a re-read for us Christians as we easily become distracted from Jesus and the gospel. The Rev. McCheyne skillfully, passionately, biblically takes you back to the only source of your Christian joy and leaves you there luxuriating in the wonderful glory of God in Christ.

**NATHAN KLINE**
Senior Pastor
Friendly Hills Church
Jamestown, North Carolina

As you would expect from Robert Murray McCheyne, this book is thoroughly theological and profoundly pastoral. He mines deep and then displays sparkling gospel gems on every page. This is a book that should be kept close and read often.

## Susan Hunt
Wife of retired pastor Gene Hunt
Former Director of Women's Ministry for the Presbyterian Church in America
Co-author with Karen Hodge of *Transformed—Life-taker to Life-giver*

Robert Murray McCheyne is one of my heroes. He only lived until 29 and was only in the ministry for a little over seven years. But in that short time he taught many (and continues to teach through his books) that our life in Christ is far more important than anything this world has to offer. In this short but powerful book, he reminds us that our joy can only be found in Christ. Much like his other works and those of his contemporaries in 19th century Scotland, this book will pierce your heart and convict your soul that nothing short of pursuing the King of kings in all things will fill you with gladness.

## Dave Furman
Senior Pastor of Redeemer Church of Dubai
Author of *Being There* and *Kiss the Wave*

He [McCheyne] preached with eternity stamped upon his brow. I think I yet can see his seraphic countenance, and hear his sweet and tender voice. I was spell-bound, and would not keep my eyes off him for a moment. He announced his text — Paul's thorn in the flesh. What a sermon! I trembled, and never felt God so near. His appeals went to my heart, and, as he spoke of the last great day in the darkening twilight, for once I began to pray.

## Duncan Matheson (1866-1944)
Scottish Evangelist and contemporary of McCheyne

# The
# Believer's
# Joy

## Robert Murray
## McCheyne

CHRISTIAN
HERITAGE

All Scripture quotations taken from the *King James Version*.

Copyright © 2018 Christian Focus Publications Ltd

paperback ISBN 978-1-5271-0148-7
epub ISBN 978-1-5271-0165-4
mobi ISBN 978-1-5271-0166-1

This edition printed in 2018
by
Christian Focus Publications Ltd
Geanies House, Fearn, Ross-shire
IV20 1TW, Scotland
www.christianfocus.com

Cover design by Daniel van Straaten
Printed and bound by Bell and Bain, Glasgow

# CONTENTS

# FOREWORD

## by
## Sinclair B. Ferguson

I regularly sit in St Peter's Free Church, Dundee, in the very room where Robert Murray McCheyne preached the sermons contained in *The Believer's Joy*, and wish it contained a recording device that could replay them. In his day the building seated somewhere over a thousand people. It must have been a deeply moving experience to be surrounded by the dense sound of their hearty unaccompanied singing of the Psalms, to experience the hushed and intense listening to the exposition of God's word by this young man in his mid-twenties, and at the end of the service to feel bowed down in holy wonder in God's presence. Here, for what must have seemed an all too short seven years, Robert McCheyne preached sermons like these which led to the conversion of many people, old and young, and to the spiritual nourishment of an even greater number.

In the absence of such recordings from the 1830s and early 1840s when McCheyne was minister, these pages provide the next best thing—the text of several sermons McCheyne prepared for the people he loved so dearly. They bear all the hallmarks of all his preaching—simplicity, clarity, directness, earnestness, Christ-centredness, and in addition a certain pathos and poetic beauty. Given that they were preached by a young man still in his mid-twenties, they reveal a heart that had grown rapidly in the grace and knowledge of Christ.

Sermons do not always transfer to the printed page, for the simple reason that preaching is never only a matter of words. As Phillips Brooks famously noted, it is 'truth through personality' and the latter does not always come through on the printed page. But with McCheyne's sermons it does. No matter what age or stage of the Christian life you may have reached, you will find yourself spiritually nourished and drawn to Christ by what you read here.

There was a time when McCheyne's name was a household word throughout the evangelical world. His friend Andrew Bonar's classic biographical work, *Memoirs and Remains of R.M. McCheyne* was part of the staple diet for Christians old and young, and provided particular encouragement and challenge to every would-be minister of the gospel. But those days have long gone, and so it may be helpful here to explain briefly who McCheyne was.

Robert Murray McCheyne was born on May 21, 1813, the youngest of five children, into a comfortable middle-class family in Edinburgh. His father was a lawyer. One sister had died before he was born. His older brother

David, also a lawyer, and a young man of deep Christian faith, died suddenly when Robert was eighteen. This led, in due season to his spiritual awakening and then to his sense of calling to the ministry of the gospel. Already an able student, he threw himself into theological studies under Thomas Chalmers and also into evangelistic and pastoral work. At the same time, he forged friendships in a small brotherhood of outstandingly able fellow-students, including Andrew Bonar (who would later accompany him on their famous visit to the Holy Land), and his brother Horatius (who would become perhaps the greatest of all Scottish hymn writers). This little brotherhood would read and study the Scriptures in their original languages and meet for discussion, prayer, mutual encouragement and evangelistic outreach. The creation of a spiritual brotherhood is a pattern that God has often used when preparing to do a fresh work of grace in the church—we may think of Calvin and his friends, or the spiritual brotherhood among the Puritans, or of the Eclectic Society in England in the 18th century. So it proved to be with McCheyne and his young friends.

Licensed to preach the gospel on July 1, 1835, McCheyne spent the next year as an assistant to the Revd John Bonar in Larbert and Dunipace. Here he learned how to preach—several times a week—began to write, and developed his life-long pattern of pastoral visitation. In the following November he was ordained and installed in the newly formed St Peter's Church in Dundee, and on his first Sunday preached on Isaiah 61:1-3 ('The Spirit of the Lord has anointed me to preach …'—a text to which he would return each year on the anniversary of his ordination).

For the next six and a half years, with various absences from his pulpit due to illness, McCheyne pointed his people to Christ, loved them, and prayed constantly for them both in public and private. Under his guidance they learned to trust and love the Saviour, to worship in Spirit and in truth, and to serve together to meet the spiritual and physical needs of the several thousand people who lived in their parish. He visited constantly, prayed much, and preached frequently. Among other things he took a special interest in children (although he was unmarried and had no children of his own) and started a Sunday School for them as well as a young people's meeting on Tuesdays that attracted as many as two hundred and fifty. He encouraged the people to gather for prayer in homes as well as weekly in the church. His midweek Bible study filled the church and sometimes overflowed.

In the Spring of 1839 McCheyne was part of a deputation sent on an exploratory mission throughout Europe en route to the Holy Land, investigating the conditions of the Jewish people. It was then that fresh spiritual fire fell on the St Peter's congregation under the preaching of a young locum minister, William Chalmers Burns. Remarkably, Burns was only recently turned twenty-four at the time. McCheyne himself seemed to have a sense that God might work in a new way in his absence. But on his return the spiritual quickening continued, and his own ministry reaped a rich harvest. One of his notebooks contains the record of hundreds of visits he personally made to people who were enquiring about Christ as a result.

Never physically strong, however, in 1843 Robert Murray McCheyne succumbed to the typhoid epidemic that was rife in the city. In twenty-nine short years, with little over a decade as a true Christian, he had burnt himself out in the service of the Saviour he so deeply and evidently loved. In the providence of God, however, his brief ministry would not only leave the mark of Christ on his congregation, but Andrew Bonar's record of it would prove to be an inspiration to countless Christians who would read his story, be challenged by the spiritual reflections in his diary, or be blessed by singing one or other his hymns (especially 'I once was a stranger to grace and to God' or 'When this passing world is done'). Throughout the intervening years students and ministers have found him a model worthy of imitating in the pursuing godliness and in 'zeal for the glory of God and a desire for the salvation of men'—the commitments made in presbyterian ordination services.

McCheyne's story is wonderfully and lovingly told by Bonar in his *Memoirs and Remains of R.M. McCheyne*[1] as well as by others—most recently by L.J. Van Valen in *Constrained by His Love*[2] and, more briefly, by David Robertson (the current minister of St Peter's) in his excellent study of McCheyne's ministry entitled *Awakening*.[3] In addition, several volumes of his sermons remain in print alongside this little work. These books can all be recommended for further reading.

Speaking of reading, the best way to benefit fully from McCheyne's sermons is to *read them out loud*—whether

1. The 1892 edition has been reprinted (Edinburgh: The Banner of Truth Trust, 1966).

2. Translated from the Dutch edition of 1993 by Laurence R Nicolson (Fearn, Tain: Christian Focus Publications), 2002.

3. Milton Keynes, Authentic Media, 2004.

to yourself or to someone else. These are *sermons*, after all; they are not essays; they were not written to be read silently but to be preached publicly. And this remains the best way to 'hear' them and feel their weight as their first hearers must have done. I believe if you do this you will be more likely to appreciate both the power of the sermons and the poetry in Robert McCheyne's soul.

Christian Focus Publications have already made available several volumes of McCheyne's sermons; we owe them a debt of gratitude for now also making *The Believer's Joy* available for a new generation of readers.

Sinclair B Ferguson

# I

# The Believer's Prayer for Divine Teaching

*'Open Thou mine eyes that I may behold wondrous things out of Thy law.'*
Psalm 119:18

The *law* of God here spoken of is the Bible. In the days of David, the Law, or the Five Books of Moses, formed the greater part of the Bible, and so the whole was often called the Law. So, in the first Psalm, 'His delight is in the law of the LORD.' At verse 97 he says, 'O how love I Thy law, it is my meditation all the day' (Ps. 119:97). And here, 'Open Thou mine eyes,' etc.

*The wondrous things* seem to be the great things of an eternal world. David had looked on the wonders of this world – he had turned his enquiring eyes upon the wonders of nature, sun, moon, and stars, mountains, trees, and rivers. He had seen many of the wonders of art; but now, he wanted to see the spiritual wonders contained in the Bible. He wanted to know about God Himself in all

His majesty, purity, and grace. He wanted to learn the way of salvation by a crucified Redeemer, and the glory that is to follow. These were the wondrous things David wanted to see.

'*Open mine eyes*' – David was not blind – his eye was not dim. He could read the Bible from end to end, and yet he felt that he needed more light. He felt that he needed to see deeper, to have the eyes of his understanding opened. He felt that if he had nothing but his own eyes and natural understanding, he would not discover the wonders which he panted to see. He wanted Divine teaching – the eye-salve of the spirit; and therefore he would not open the Bible without this prayer 'Open Thou mine eyes!'

## I. We Need Divine Teaching to see the Wonders of the Bible.

This is plain from the few that are converted under the preaching of the Gospel. 'Many are called but few are chosen,' has been the rule from the earliest times. If human teaching could reveal the wonders of the Bible, then all who are taught by man would believe; but this is far from being the case. Noah was a preacher of righteousness; alas, with how few did he prevail. Isaiah complains, 'Who hath believed our report, and to whom is the arm of the Lord revealed?' In what plaintive strains did Jeremiah preach, and yet he is forced to cry, 'Woe is me, my mother, that thou hast borne me a man of strife and a man of contention to the whole earth.' And in another place he complains, that there was not one man in the whole of Jerusalem seeking the truth. When our Lord was on earth as a minister, how many thousands heard Him on the mountains of Galilee, and by the seashore, and in the streets of Jerusalem. On the last day of the feast He stood and cried when there were thousands present, and yet after He rose from the dead five hundred brethren were all that could be gathered.

When Paul preached at Athens, he stood in the midst of Mars Hill, among thousands of the most acute people that ever were in this world, yet most of them mocked, some put him off to another day; and scarcely more than one man and one woman believed.

So now, many a faithful minister feels the same. There is much preaching, little saving. A godly minister in his lifetime may hold forth the word of life to many thousand souls, yet he may go to his rest with but a few for his crown of joy in the day of the Lord. Think how many faithful ministers there are in the world – how many millions of Bibles read – how many faithful sermons preached – how many teachers – how many children taught the Catechism and the Word of God – how many millions of pious books spreading abroad the truth as it is in Jesus; and yet how few are saved. Oh cry, 'Open Thou mine eyes that I may behold wondrous things out of Thy law!' (Ps. 119:18)

## II. God is the Only Effectual Teacher.

1. Because He only knows those wondrous things as they really are. Ministers have but a glimpse of those wondrous things, and it is no wonder they cannot teach them effectually. They see but a very little of sin, the mountains of guilt, the shortness of time, the depth of hell, the love of God. They see but little into the heart of Jesus, His amazing atonement, His free righteousness. It is not once in a hundred sermons that we speak rightly of Christ. Books also are infinitely imperfect. The best of books are but sparks from the Bible, mingled with human darkness.

– But God knows, 'all is naked and open before the eyes of Him with whom we have to do' (Heb. 4:13). He knows our sins, the mountains that are over us. He knows the shortness of life. The awful depths of hell are naked to His view. He knows his own love, the glory of Jesus. The Father delights to contemplate Christ, His fullness, freeness, fitness. 'No man knoweth the Son but the Father, and no man knoweth the Father but the Son, and he to whom the Son will reveal him' (Matt. 11:27). Do any of you feel your need of divine teaching? Oh, run unto Him; cry, 'Open Thou mine eyes!'

2. Because He only can teach the heart. Man can speak to the ear, to the understanding, to the memory; God alone to the heart. The reason why human teaching cannot convey light to the soul is that the heart is dead; the natural heart hates God, and everything that comes from God, and therefore, when the truth is presented, the heart draws the mind away from it. But when God teaches, He breaks the heart, and it melts; He awakens concern in the dead heart, so that the person runs to hear the word preached; He awakens desire after Christ, and salvation by Christ; He makes the soul willing to be saved in God's way. None can teach like God. He can teach a little child as easily as the oldest man; nay, He can teach an idiot as easily as the wisest man. Some hearing me have seen this.

Oh, what encouragement is here to little children. Do not think it is above you. What encouragement to poor ignorant creatures, to those who cannot read. Oh, cry to God 'Open Thou mine eyes!'

## III.   WHAT IS DIVINE TEACHING?

1. *What it is not.* It is not mere head-knowledge of the Bible. Many have great head-knowledge of the Bible, have

read it through and through – studied it all. They know the catechism well and have a just notion of systematic Divinity. Some have much book-knowledge, have a relish for the best books; are great judges of sermons; are able to distinguish an evangelical ministry – yet all this may be without a spark of divine teaching. Ah, is there such an one here? What need have you to cry, 'Open Thou mine eyes!'

It is not a sight of Christ with the bodily eyes. Many saw Him on earth who never were the better for it. Yea, thousands saw Him hanging on the cross, who only wagged their heads at Him in scorn. Every one shall see Him soon, coming in the clouds of heaven, and yet most will only wail because of Him.

Neither is it any vision or fancied revelation of Christ. It is not any impression made on the imagination. Some may fancy they see Christ hanging on the cross, or smiling upon them; they may fancy they see a bright form. This is not the teaching of God; it is infinitely inferior.

Neither is it revealing some truths that are not in the Bible. The wonders which God reveals are all in the Law.

Some may fancy that certain words are borne in upon their mind, as, 'I have redeemed thee; thou are Mine' – 'I have loved thee and died for thee.' But this is not revealing the wonders out of the Law. This is vastly inferior, and is probably mere delusion.

2. *What it is.* – It is giving the soul a sense of the wondrous excellency of the gospel way of salvation, 'That I may see wondrous things.' Before conversion, the man read the same words in the Bible, repeated the same truths in the Catechism, but he saw no wonder in them; now he discovers the wondrous nature of them. A man looking at

the sun in a mist, may see nothing wonderful; but if the mist be drawn away, and the sun shines out gloriously, the man is filled with a wondrous sense of the glory. So with the glory of Christ, that better Sun. The Man is filled with a wondrous sense of the glory of the person of Christ; He is seen to be 'The Rose of Sharon, and the Lily of the Valley.' He is filled with a sense of the wondrous wisdom and peace in the way of salvation by Jesus Christ. If there were ten thousand other ways, he prefers *this* to all, giving glory to God, and safety to his soul.

Beloved, have you had this teaching? If you have, bless God for it, 'Blessed is the man whom Thou choosest.' Pray for more of it. David could not be satisfied.

### IV. Marks of Divine Teaching.

1. *It causes souls to cleave sweetly to Christ.* – This is the sure mark of all who are taught of God. Before, they were quite puzzled about coming to Christ, believing on Him, closing with Him. But now, they see no difficulties at all; they cannot but believe. Just as one cannot doubt that the sun is shining when they see it, so they cannot doubt the word of Christ, or their interest in Him. They forsake their own righteousness for ever – push themselves aside as condemned, deny themselves, 'count all things but loss for the excellency of the knowledge of Christ Jesus' (Phil. 3:8). They take up the cross daily; anything that hides Christ they let it go.

2. *It sanctifies.* – Human teaching does not. A man may have the head-knowledge of an angel, and the heart of a devil. Human teaching civilises, it does not christianise. But this sweet teaching of God sanctifies. 'Beholding, as

in a glass, the glory of the Lord, we are changed into the same image, from glory to glory, even as by the Spirit of the Lord' (2 Cor. 3:18). With His stripes we are healed;' and the sanctified one cries, 'God forbid that I should glory, save in the cross of our Lord Jesus Christ, by whom the world is crucified to me, and I unto the world' (Gal. 6:14).

3. *It gives desire that others should be taught.* – Not so human teaching. Knowledge puffeth up. A man who has much mere human teaching is proud, and loves to show his superiority; but the heaven-taught soul delights to obey the command of Jesus, 'Go home to thy friends, and tell them how great things the Lord hath done for thee' (Mark 5:19) and He wishes that all the world would come to know Him who is so sweet, so full, so free. He prays, 'Open Thou their eyes, that they may behold wondrous things out of Thy law!'

So you, dear friends in Jesus, go home and ask, what can I do for Christ? How may I teach by words, by looks, by deeds, 'by righteousness, godliness, faith, love, patience, meekness?' How may I teach by letters, by books, by tracts? Dark, cold, and powerless in themselves, yet, filled with the Spirit of God, they may convey life, and light and gladness, into thousands of dwellings. The smallest tract may be the stone in David's sling. In the hands of Christ, it may bring down a giant soul.

# 2

# THE BELIEVER'S JOY IN GOD

*'We joy in God.'* [1]
Romans 5:11

The phrase with which this verse commences – 'And not only so, but also' – shows plainly that we are now about to enter upon a higher grade of the believer's privileges. We have arrived at the summit of the climax of the believer's joys. In the first two verses Paul speaks of peace, access, and joyful hope of glory, as the first and immediate privileges of the believer. From the third to the tenth verse he speaks of the joy of the believer occasioned by tribulations. But now he leads us deeper into the heart of the believer, and reveals to us his highest privilege – his sweetest joy.

*We joy in God through our Lord Jesus Christ.* And surely this privilege is more than all that went before. Peace with

---

1. The verse is '... we also joy in God ...

God is a blessed thing, but it does not imply that the heart is burning with intense joy and love in view of a reconciled God. Access to His favour is a blessed thing; but it only implies liberty of coming before Him with acceptance. Joy in hope of glory is a blessed thing; but it is in the very nature of it a happiness whose object is unenjoyed and afar off. Joy in tribulation, again, is a blessed thing; but it is a happiness which can only be enjoyed upon the earth. It is a joy, too, in spite of misery – a perfecting, but surely not a perfect joy. But *Joy in God* is the most blessed thing of all. This is the third heaven of the believer's privileges – a joy which all the redeemed are sharing with angels – a joy begun in this world, made perfect in glory.

Oh! my believing friends, how little do we live, in this age of dead and heartless Christianity, like those who have God for their present portion – like those who, amid the full tide of prosperity, or the low ebbings of adversity, have a constant and unfailing springing up of this holy joy within. There are flowers which always turn their faces to the sun and follow it in it's daily journey, ever looking towards it with most loving diligence. Though the storm may make them droop for a little, still they point to the one beloved orb. And so should the believer, whether his sky be clear, or covered with clouds; God – his God – his reconciled, reconciling God – is the sun in his heaven to which his face is ever directed, and from which his beams of gladness ever descend. Who can tell the holy joy thus poured into his cup! When he goes forth to his morning toil, who can tell how the sunlight of the countenance of a God whom he loves is shed around all his paths? – how the cheerful step and open brow that graced the green sward of primeval paradise are restored to man, whilst he whispers in his own heart, 'O Lord, Thou hast searched and known me. Thou knowest my downsitting and mine uprising; Thou understandest my thought afar off. Thou compassest my path and my lying down, and art acquainted with all my ways' (Psalm 139:1-3). And when he comes home weary, and lays down his head on his pillow to rest, after the fatigues of a hard wrought day, who can tell the calm delight that steals over him while he whispers to his reconciled God and Father, 'How precious also are thy thoughts unto me, O God! how great is the sum of them. If I should count them, they are more in number than the sand. When I awake, I am still with thee.'

Let us consider several of the Springs of this joy.

### *The believer joys in God because*

### He is Omniscient.

He only can say, I am glad that God knows all my past history, that He hath been witness of my long ungodliness, of the sins of my heart – of my tongue – of my hand; for this makes me sure that the Saviour He has sent and offers to me is a Saviour that answers my case. Just as the sick man is glad when the physician seems to understand perfectly the whole of the disease, when he has probed to the bottom of every wound, and knows every symptom of the malady, so am I glad that God is hourly witness of my diseased heart, that He knows every one of my indwelling corruptions; because this good Physician will give me grace according to my need. He will not suffer me to be tempted above that I am able to bear. He will perfect His strength in my weakness, so that as my day is, so shall my strength be.

*The believer joys in God because*

## HE IS ALMIGHTY.

So long as we are unconverted, the Almightiness of God should be terrible to us. If you cast your eye over the dwellings of the ungodly, it is quite true you see them all living in perfect security. And you may often see them filled with admiration of Jehovah's power. They will stand and gaze beside the foaming cataract – they will stand and listen while Jehovah is rending the heavens with His thunder – they will gaze with admiration when He is guiding the moon across the sun's golden path, and they are not reminded of the time when the sun shall be darkened and the moon not give her light. But just imagine for a moment that the eyes of all unconverted men were opened to see the situation in which they stand. Oh! what doleful cries of agony and terror would rise from every dwelling, when they saw that the Almightiness of Jehovah is all ready to be let loose upon them, body and soul, for ever. We would hear something like the cries which pierced the heavens when the flood came upon the world – we would hear something like the cries which shall one day soon rise from every unconverted heart, when Christ shall come in the clouds, and all kindreds of the earth shall wail because of Him.

If sinners could but see that there is nothing but the hand of God staying back the fury of His anger, and that only for a time – that there is nothing but the good plea-sure of God keeping any of them out of hell – if they could but see that the same hand which balances the earth upon nothing, the hand that wields the thunderbolt, the hand that darkens the sun with ominous eclipse – that that very hand is pledged to destroy every Christless soul, oh! who would be able to bear the sight? The stoutest hearted among the wicked would find their knees becoming weak as water – they would cry 'to the mountains and rocks, Fall on us, and hide us from the face of Him that sitteth on the throne, and from the wrath of the Lamb' (Rev. 6:16). The terribleness of wrath is always in proportion to the might of the being who is angry. The wrath of a child is contemptible, because it has no power to put it in execution. The wrath of the lion is terrible, because it excels in strength. When the sea is lashed into fury by the storm, it is fearful to look upon it, there is so much power in every one of the surges that dash upon the rocks. The wrath of the king, says the Bible, is terrible. But, ah! what must the wrath of God be – the King of kings, for He is almighty. When the Almightiness of God is roused up to destroy, oh who can stand? Who can tell the dreadfulness of being *trodden in the wine-press of the fierceness of the wrath of Almighty God.*

But the believer exults in the thought of 'abiding under the shadow of the Almighty' (Ps. 91:1). 'Thou shalt have thy delight in the Almighty' (Job 22:26). 'I will say of the Lord, He is my refuge and my fortress: my God; in Him will I trust' (Ps. 91:2). 'For in the time of trouble He shall hide me in His pavilion: in the secret of His tabernacle shall He hide me; He shall set me upon a rock' (Ps. 27:5).

## *The believer joys in God because*

### HE IS JUST.

So long as we are unconverted, the justice of God should be terrible to us, for it is pledged to destroy us; and accordingly, this is the attribute of God which of all others is vilified and opposed by the natural heart. Regarding Him in the light of a tender Father, some think He is far too lenient to look with any eye but one of compassion on their weaknesses and sins, forgetting that He is also the Lawgiver and Ruler of the universe. Others would grant Him to be a Lawgiver and Sovereign, but then so very great and exalted above His subjects, that He would not stoop to punish every sin. The Gospel alone tells us that every idle word God will bring into judgment – that all men are on a coming day to be judged in righteousness – that no sin can ever go unpunished – that God can by no means clear the guilty – that heaven and earth shall pass away before one jot or one tittle of the law pass away.

'Bless the Lord, O my soul,' exclaims the justified believer, 'I have found a perfect righteousness in the life and death of my glorified Lord. In His death I have borne all the penalties of the outraged law – in His life I have fulfilled all the demands of that holy law. The heavens are not clean in His sight, but I in Christ am clean. The angels He charged with folly, but in Jesus I am more righteous than angels.'

### *The believer joys in God because*

## HE IS LOVE.

This is the sum of the reasons why the believer joys in God – this is the oil which feeds the lamp of his joy. It is the fuel which keeps the fire of his joy for ever kindled, and for ever blazing toward heaven. He joys in God's past love – in His present love – in His love which is to come.

He looks back to his condition when he was a child of wrath, even as others, and he remembers that then God first loved him. It was when he was in his blood that God said unto him, Live (see Ezekiel 16:6). He did not choose Christ, but Christ chose him. Oh, who but the believer can tell the wondering joy that sparkles in his bosom when he looks back on this the compassionate love of God. – How marvellous that God should have sought me when I was seeking sin – that Christ should have shed His blood for me when I saw no beauty in Him to desire Him – that the Spirit should have awakened me when so many around are slumbering. Oh, my believing friends, you know what I mean – you feel the joy which I cannot describe!

*The believer joys in God because*

## GOD NOW LOVES HIM.

To one who has been long confined to a sick-room, there is something unspeakably refreshing in the cheering beams of the summer sun; and so to the soul that has been all its life under wrath, there is something unspeakably joyful in abiding under the beams of God's reconciled countenance.

There are two things which make it peculiarly delightful –

1.  That we are accepted through imputed righteousness. There is something inexpressibly pleasing to a justified mind, to know that God has all the honour of our salvation, and we have none – to know that God's honour is not violated, but on the contrary, shines more illustrious – to know that God's law is not injured, but magnified and made honourable – to know that we are safe, and God has all the glory. Oh! this is a blessed assurance.

2.  That God will keep us always in a state of acceptance – that it will continue. How often are worldly joys embittered by the thought that they will not last till

tomorrow's sun. Like spring flowers – the sweetest aye the fleetest. But though our sense of acceptance should fall away and leave us comfortless, we know that God will put His fear in us, and not suffer us to go away from Him.

Has God begun a work in your heart? Oh, be glad in the Lord, for He will finish it. Mountains may lie in your way; but He will make the mountains skip like rams, and the little hills like lambs.

Has God carried you through the Red Sea? Be sure He will bring you to the green pastures and still waters.

### *The believer joys in God because*

### GOD WILL LOVE HIM FOR EVER.

'They shall be Mine, saith the Lord of hosts, in that day when I make up My jewels' (Mal. 3:17). Oh! if it be joyful to look back on God's wondrous love that is past – if it be joyful to bask in the beams of His reconciled countenance now, what will it be to joy in God's love in eternity, when all those full treasures of love are flowing out of that heart towards us – when we are His own jewels in that day. Oh! if He be so precious to us here in the wilderness, that ofttimes the wilderness blossoms as the rose – if He feeds us and leads us so when we are pilgrims and strangers, what will He not do for us when He brings us home to Himself. If the presence of His Spirit in our heart be so precious now, oh! what will it be to recline on the heart of that God who is Love.

Dear unconverted friends, I do not say you know anything of this joy; but I do say, that if you do not know something of it before you die, you will never come to know it after.

## 'ABBA, FATHER'
### Galatians 4:6

No natural man cries, 'Abba.' It is not the cry of nature. Children cry 'Father' to their earthly parents. It is one of the first things they learn. They do not thus call upon God; but when one comes to Christ, and feels the Father's smile, the Father's arms, the Father's love, he cries 'Abba.'

Often it is little more than a cry. Many of God's children are not fluent in prayer. They have not many words.

Often they can only look up, and cry, 'Father.' A soul in Christ can cry, 'Father!' This runs through all he says to God, 'Abba.' 'In the multitude of words there wanteth not sin' (Prov. 10:19) but this one word is the believer's prayer. 'Abba.'

# 3

# Laodicea: or the Lukewarm Professor

Revelation 3:14-22

Near the coast of Asia Minor stand the splendid ruins of ancient Ephesus. The remains of the Temple of Diana are still seen, and on the side of the hill the immense theatre still remains, where Demetrius gathered the multitude, and where they shouted, 'Great is Diana of the Ephesians.' It was there Paul laboured for three years night and day with tears. But they left their first love, and now the candlestick is taken out of its place, and there is not so much as one inhabitant of the desolate Ephesus, it stands a monument of a Church that left its first love.

About a hundred miles further into the country are to be seen the ruins of another city, almost completely buried by an earthquake. The ruins are of vast extent, and none but the wild beasts of the desert dwell there. It is all that remains of Laodicea. Often Paul wrestled for it in prayer – again and again he sent his epistles to it. But now it stands a monument of a Church having the form of godliness, and denying the power of it. Ephesus affords a warning to all of you, dear brethren, who, having received the grace of God, are going back, leaving your first love. Laodicea affords a warning to those of you who have the outward form and appearance of Christians, but to whom the truth has never come with saving power. 'I know thy works, that thou art neither cold nor hot' (Rev. 3:15).

Let us look at the

STATE OF LAODICEA; NEITHER COLD NOR HOT –
LUKEWARM; and we shall see –

### 1. WHAT THEY HAD.

*They had all the forms of a Church.* They had an angel of the Church (that is, a minister), on whose ministry they awaited; or Christ sends them this message through their minster. They had a house of prayer. They had Bibles. They had epistles of Paul written to them, as you will see in Col. 4:16. They had had faithful ministers labouring among them, as Epaphras of whom Paul bears record that he had a great zeal for them in Laodicea, Col. 4:13. Paul often prayed for them, and Epaphras also laboured on his knees. No doubt they had the word faithfully preached, and sat down at the Lord's table, and yet for all that the True Witness says, 'I know thy works, that thou are neither cold nor hot.'

Oh, brethren, is it not the same with many of you? You also have the forms of a Church – you also have a minister set over you in the Lord, on whose ministry you wait – you have Bibles, and sermons preached to you as often as you please – you have had letters addressed to you, and ministers striving for you on their knees, – and yet for all that the Faithful and True Witness may say of many of you, 'I know thy works, that thou art neither cold nor hot.' Outward privileges do not make a Christian. Dear friend, I tremble for most of you, lest all you have be the 'name to live.'

*They had much head knowledge.* There is reason to think that the Church of Laodicea had a clear knowledge of the Gospel. As I have said, Paul seems often to have written to them, and Epaphras no doubt laboured with great diligence among them; for a minister that is fervent on his knees is always mighty when he labours among a people; so that it is probable the men of Laodicea were well instructed in the things of the Gospel – and yet for all that, the Lord Jesus whose eyes reach to the heart said, 'I know thy works, that thou art neither cold nor hot.'

Oh, brethren, I tremble for you. How many of you have great head knowledge of the Bible – have read it all – studied it all – learned much of it by heart! How many of you know the Catechism well – have a just knowledge of divinity – are able to explain the covenants, and to reconcile election of God and the free will of man! Many of you have great knowledge of good books – of Boston, and Willison, and Flavel, 'of whom the world was not worthy.' Many are great judges of sermons. You know well a fitly arranged discourse – you can discriminate well between gospel and legal preaching, – and yet for all this you may have an unbroken unsanctified heart. Jesus may be saying of you, 'I know thy works, that thou are neither cold nor hot.' I know there have been many ministers, who, like the Gibeonites, have been hewers of wood and drawers of water unto all the congregation (Josh. 9:21) – like the fingerpost which points the way, itself standing immoveable. I suppose Judas had some knowledge of divinity, and could speak well, and yet he was a devil. I believe the devils have a clear knowledge of divinity, and yet they only 'tremble.'

Ah, brethren, I tremble for you. Unsanctified knowledge will be like a millstone to sink your soul.

## 2. WHAT THEY HAD NOT.

*They had no discovery of sin.* 'Thou sayest, I am rich and increased with goods, and have need of nothing' (Rev. 3:17). Here was the spring and root of all their lukewarmness. They had ministers, and Bibles, and sacraments. They had much knowledge of divinity, but they had never been convinced of sin. When the Comforter comes, His first work in the heart is to convince of sin; but they had never been convinced of sin – the work of the Spirit had never been begun in their hearts. They had never seen themselves wretched and miserable – never seen the awful curse under which every unconverted soul lies – the deadness, corruption, and depravity of their hearts, that would not turn to Christ without divine power. They never knew their poverty, that they had nothing before God. They never knew their blindness, that the veil was over their hearts; nor their nakedness, that they were exposed to the wrath of an angry God.

Ah! this is the reason they were neither cold nor hot – this is the reason they could sit unmoved under the awakening, affectionate sermons of Epaphras and unmelted by the tender epistles of Paul. Beloved! Here is the spring of your lukewarmness. You say, 'I am rich.' You do not know your guilt – you do not know the plague of your own heart. Oh, if God would take the veil away, and shew you this day your wretchedness – if He were to shew your heart, how hard it is – how insensible – how dead, this would be no longer a lukewarm Church. You would no longer be formalists – you would go, and weep as you go, Oh, that God would send us such a time!

*They had no relish for divine things.* The life of a believer is one of keen relish for divine things. Whether Christ be present or absent, the soul has a keen edge for Christ. 'I sat down under His shadow with great delight, and His fruit was sweet to my taste' (Song 2:3). There is no lukewarmness there. 'I sought Him whom my soul loveth: I sought Him but I found Him not. I will rise now and go about the city, in the streets, and in the broad ways I will seek Him whom my soul loveth: I sought Him, but I found Him not' (Song 3:1-2). Still there is the same hungering and thirsting after Christ. Now the men of Laodicea never felt this.

Dear friends, how is it with you? Have you sat under His shadow with great delight? Is His fruit sweet to your taste? Can you lay your hand on your heart and say, you know what it is to have a heart breaking with longing towards Christ? Does your conversation savour of Christ? Do you relish secret prayer? Can you lay your hand on your heart and say, you find delight on your knees? Do you love family prayer?

*They had no fervency in Christ's cause.* When a soul is really united to Christ, it is fervent in Christ's cause. 'The multitude of them that believed were of one heart and of one soul' (Acts 4:32). No longer selfish, cold, and calculating. Is Christ's cause 'put to the worse?' Does Israel turn its back upon his enemies? Then that man lies down on his face before God. Are sinners added to the Lord? That man sees the grace of God and is glad. Are efforts making to extend the Redeemer's kingdom? That man is ready with heart and hand – with all he has – to help it forward. Oh, what a lovely sight is a real believer in Jesus! Like Barnabas, he sells his property and lays it at the apostles' feet (see Acts 4:37). He is a ray from the Sun of Righteousness. His heart is filled with the grace of the Lord Jesus.

Beloved! how is it with you? Are you willing to spend and be spent in this blessed service – to make greater efforts than you have ever yet made in Christ's service? Ah! how many say, No. 'I know thy works, that thou art neither cold nor hot.'

*Let us now see*

## WHAT CHRIST SAYS OF SUCH.

'*I would thou wert cold or hot.*' A lukewarm soul is more offensive to Christ than one that has no appearance of goodness at all. Observe, these are the words of the True and Faithful Witness, who sees to the bottom of men's hearts; by whom actions are weighed, and who cannot lie. 'I would thou wert cold.' There are many who are quite cold in divine things; the unbaptised heathen – the ungodly multitude who come not near a church, and who never sit down at a sacrament – those who do not profess to be God's people at all. Oh, formalist. Christ says, I would thou wert one of these! When Christ was on earth, He spoke far more dreadful words to the Pharisees than to the publicans and sinners. And so does He now in heaven. The reason is this, Laodicea sinned against greater light than others. They had the Gospel preached, and yet

were lukewarm under it. Oh, brethren, this is your condemnation. You have more light than the wretched families around you, who have no place in the house of God.
You have the most awful truths pressed upon you, and yet
you sit dead and heartless under all. Your sin is committed
in the house of God, in His very presence. So, here He tells
the Laodiceans,

'*I will spue thee out of my mouth.*' There are none who
will perish so miserably as those of you, dear brethren,
who have companied with us from the first day even till
now – who have cleaved to this Church through good report and bad report – who are among our most faithful
and regular adherents – who would perhaps fight for your
minister – but, alas, have got an unsaved soul.

Your wrath will be all the greater. Christ Himself will
cast you away. You shall be a castaway. You will need to
give account of every sermon you heard, and every impression you resisted. Ah, it will be fearful reckoning!
I shall be a swift witness against you. I can honestly say,
I have been affectionately desirous of you, that you should
be my joy and crown. But I shall be a swift witness against
most. I preached the Gospel to that man, I told him of his
sin and misery; but he was neither cold nor hot. Let him
be a castaway.

Your disappointment will be terrible. I know well, dear
brethren, that you expect nothing else but to ascend up to
glory with those that are saved. Though you have no marks
of the regenerated nature, you are easy. 'Thou sayest, I am
rich and increased with goods, and have need of nothing.'
Beloved, think, before it be too late, what good will it do
you to cling round the ark, if you enter not in. Reflect what
a sad thing it will be to be separated from Christ's sheep,

and put at His left hand. What a dreadful thing it will be to have journeyed so long with us, and then to a situation in which to be lukewarm? If your own opinions are true, then how can you be parted. Some of you have sat down at every Lord's table with us, have been present at almost every sermon, joined in almost every prayer. And no doubt you think to enter into the same rest with God's people in this place. Ah, what a dreadful mistake when you find the door shut! You will knock and say, 'Lord, Lord, open to us; Thou hast eaten and drunk in our presence, and taught in our streets.' And He will say, 'Depart, I know you not.'

## REASONS AGAINST LUKEWARMNESS.

*Reflect for a moment on the solemn opinions you hold.* I suppose there is not a man in this church but holds it as his opinion that you must be converted or perish, that every one that is not born again is on the road to hell. Ah! think for a moment, is that opinion true? And are you unconverted? Then you are on the road to hell.Are your children – your companions unconverted? Then they are on the road to hell. The waves of the burning lake are below your feet. Is that a situation in which to be lukewarm? If your own opinions are true, then how can you be easy? Oh, brethren, do not let Satan delude you any more. How long are you to be cheated by him?

*See how busy Satan is.* He is not lukewarm. Your adversary the devil goeth about as a roaring lion. There is no lukewarmness in heaven, and none in hell. Devils and damned souls are not lukewarm. It is only you, unconverted sinner. Satan is day and night striving to keep you in your deep slumber.

I feel deeply persuaded, brethren, that some of you are at this moment under his power. 'If our Gospel be hid, it is hid to them that are lost' (2 Cor. 4:3). In some he plucks away the seed as soon as it is sown. Some he makes say, 'when I have a convenient season I will call for thee' (Acts 24:25). Some he stirs up like Festus, to think the preacher mad – 'Thou art beside thyself, much learning doth make thee mad' (Acts 26:24). Oh, brethren, he walketh about as a 'roaring lion.' Shall he be so anxious to devour, and you so careless about your own soul?

*See how urgent Christ is – 'Behold I stand at the door.'* Well might he say, 'Behold!' Although the lukewarm soul is the vilest in the world in the eye of Christ, yet hear how He pleads, – 'I counsel thee to buy of me gold tried in the fire, that thou mayest be rich; and white raiment that though mayest be clothed, and that the shame of thy nakedness do not appear; and anoint thine eyes with eye-salve, that thou mayest see' (Rev. 3:18). 'Behold I stand at the door and knock' (Rev. 3:20). Beloved, if the terrors of wrath will not drive you, shall the melting love of Christ not draw you? Is it possible that the Son of God cares more for your soul than you do for your own? Is He so urgent and you so cold? Do you not feel, in providences, in sermons and in countless ways, that Christ is indeed standing, knocking, at some of your doors, it may be, for fifty years? Oh, brethren, if you do perish, it is because you would not be saved. Let your lukewarm soul be roused. Sure all is not well with it. Perhaps this is your day of mercy. 'Zaccheus, make haste and come down, for to-day I must abide at thy house' (Luke 19:5).

# 4

# The Song to Jesus

*'Unto Him that loved us and washed us from our sins in His own blood, and hath made us kings and priests unto God and His Father; to Him be glory and dominion for ever and ever. Amen.'*
Revelation 1:5-6

Some have thought this to be one of the songs of heaven. They have thought that, even before John's eye penetrated into the wonders of the upper world, its song of joy and ecstasy burst upon his ear – 'Unto Him that loved us.' This is evidently a mistake. It is the song of John – banished – poor – in trial and tribulation – an exiled man upon a lonely rock of the sea – a man who had his heaven begun on earth: 'Unto Him that loved us.' It has got the fragrance and melody of heaven about it.

Believers, do not fear a suffering lot. Do not fear though you be taken to a lone sickbed, or a lone rock dashed by the eternal waves of ocean. If you really know Jesus, and have tasted and seen the grace this is in Christ, you may begin the song now, 'Unto Him that loved us' – the song of a redeemed soul.

*The song invites us to consider,*

## What Christ hath done for us.

He '*loved us*' from all eternity with electing love. When He appointed the foundations of the earth, His delights were 'with the sons of men.' (Prov. 8:31) But on some He set special love. (Eph. 1:4, 5; Jer. 1:5).

Romans 9:13, 'Jacob have I loved, but Esau have I hated.' He has loved some of us who were no better than devils, no better than Hindus, no better than others in our house or family – yet He *loved us*. He has planned our salvation – ordered all the steps of it – written our names in His Book of life. O, how wonderful that Christ should love *any*. The heart of an unconverted man is so frightful, so revolting, has got such depths of sin, it is amazing He should love *any*.

Another wonder is, that when He loved any, He *loved me*. Every believer knows more evil of himself than of any other. He knows that he is the chief of sinners, and therefore he feels, what an infinite wonder that He loved *me*. The woman of Samaria could say, He *loved me*; the thief upon the cross, He *loved me*; Zaccheus, He *loved me*; and we may say the same.

Another wonder is, *What He bore in time for us*. He left heaven for us. 'Greater love hath no man than this, that a man lay down his life for his friends' (John 15:13). Jesus had His eye on the garden and the cross when He said this. John had seen Him, 'stedfastly set His face to go to Jerusalem,' – had seen Him 'in an agony – and His sweat as it were great drops of blood.' He had seen Him bound, spit upon, buffeted. He had seen Him nailed to the cross. He had seen His crown of thorns, – bleeding, dying, – the darkness, and this was what he learned from it, He loved us. He saw Him bearing our sins in His own body on the tree, standing in our place, bearing our shame, made a curse for us, made our sin; and this was what he learned, He *loved us*. If you have looked to Christ as thus suffering and dying, then you may say the same.

Another wonder is, *How He followed our soul*. Christ seems to be nearer at one time than another. Still, He seeks us all our life. When the sheep went astray, the shepherd came to seek it. So Christ *seeks* every soul He finds. *None come to Jesus unsought*. It was this John remembered. 'How I wearied Him by my sins, hardness of heart, ungodliness, and unbelief. He sent John the Baptist, He sent providence. He came to the sea of Galilee and sought me. He came to Jordan. He invited me to follow Him. When I wearied of Him, He came to me again at Galilee.'

So every one of you that has been saved. Jesus has tracked you, you have heard His footsteps, you have wearied Him with your sins, yet He followed. He sent ministers, providences, sickness. He knocked at the door – He waited long, 'My head is filled with dew, and my locks with the drops of night' (Song 5:2). Oh! surely you have cause to say, '*Unto Him that loved me*.'

But besides all this, He hath '*washed us from our sins in His own blood*.' There is nothing so defiling as our sins. Every one now redeemed was once all stained and defiled with sin – was once plunged in the miry clay. John Bunyan says, 'An unconverted man is the most *doleful* of all creatures.' One walking by the sea, said, 'My heart would pollute all that ocean.' Sin is an infinite evil. It leaves a mark on the soul that nothing human can wipe away. Oh! pray for a discovery of the loathsomeness of sin.

One thing is greater, the blood of Jesus His own blood, the blood of the Lamb. As the waters were higher than the highest mountains, so His blood can cover the highest sins. Where sin abounded grace did much more abound. It is atoning blood.

'There is a fountain fill'd with blood,
Drawn from Immanuel's veins,
And sinners plunged beneath that flood
Lost all their guilty stains'

He '*washed us*.' The fountain open will do no good unless we be washed in it. He washes all His own. Not only opens the fountain, but plunges them in. Oh! the unspeakable grace of Jesus. He begins and ends. 'God's justice and a sinful soul may embrace through this blood.'

But an unappropriated Christ is no Christ to me. If the Israelite had not put the blood on his door, he would have died. Is the blood of Jesus on the portals of your heart? Has He washed you from your sins?

Some think that Jesus loved them, though He has not washed them. Vain hope: it will perish. Some think they can wash without blood – by their tears and amendment. John Bunyan was always anxious to have sin taken off in the right way. 'I found that unless guilt of conscience was taken off the *right* way, a man grew rather worse for the loss of his trouble. Lord, let it not go off my heart but in the *right* way, by the blood of Christ, For that scripture did lie much upon me "Without shedding of blood is no remission."' (Heb. 9:22).

Oh! take care, dear friends. Some would wash, and then come; get rid of their sins, and then come to Jesus. But every one whom Christ finds is unwashed – vile – '*in their sins*.'

But still more; He hath '*made us kings and priests.*' By nature we are slaves to sin and priests to Satan. But when Christ washes the soul, He makes us kings and priests to God and His Father. These two are united in the Christian, two of the greatest offices in the world. They were united in Melchisedek. He was king of Salem, and the priest of the Most High God. They are united also in Christ. He is a priest for ever after the order of Melchisedek. He shall sit and rule a priest upon his throne. He has the linen robe of the priesthood, and the golden girdle of the king. So it is true of every one united to Christ – 'He hath made us kings and priests.'

John was at this time in Patmos, a slave. Some think he was working in the mines: underground, perhaps, loaded with a chain. And yet he says, He hath made me a king. This is true of every Christian in two respects.

He is a king in the *vastness of his possessions*. Kings of olden time had immense possessions. Of one it is said, 'the sun never set on his dominions.' Solomon gathered all the peculiar treasures of kings. But a soul united to Jesus has more. He has got the pearl of great price, the clothing of wrought gold. He has God's loving-kindness, which is better than life. He can look on the hills and valleys and resplendent rivers, and say, 'My father made them all.' 'All things are yours – whether Paul, or Apollos, or Cephas, or the world, or life, or death, or things present, or things to come; all are yours.' 'Having nothing, and yet possessing all things' (2 Cor. 6:10).

He has the *power of a king*. He has the kingly spirit of Christ. 'Uphold me with thy free Spirit' (Ps. 51:12). *He has power over his own soul*. Once he was the slave of sin. He obeyed sin, and was its slave. But now he has a new spirit within him, so that he overcomes himself. This is more than if he took a city.

He has got power *over the world.* He was once its slave. He yielded to its nod. He followed in the train – yielded to its pleasures – was bound by its silken bands. The world's dread laugh, its witching smile, enchain many souls. But now he is made free.

He has got power *over the Devil.* Once he was like the maniac – led captive by Satan at his will; sometimes driven into the fire – sometimes into the water. But when Jesus, the stronger than he, comes, He snatches thy soul out of his grasp. He makes us tread upon the lion and the adder.

Dear friends, this is what Jesus now offers – not only to wash you, but to make you kings – to give you peace now, and glory after – to make you rule over your spirit now, and rule over the nations afterwards. To give you a crown of righteousness – a crown of life – a crown of glory.

And further, He made us '*priests to God and his Father.*' A natural man is a priest of Satan. He offers continual sacrifice to the god of this world. Time, health, body, soul, are all sacrifice to the god of this world. But when Jesus saves, He makes him a priest to God.

A priest *in access.* The priests always came into the holy place; the High-priest once in the year into the holiest of all (Lev. 16:2). But now we are bid to draw near, to lean on the breast of Jesus, to come boldly to the throne of grace.

A priest *in offering up our heart.* The priests used to slay the lambs upon the altar, so we offer up a broken heart, (Ps. 51:17). A heart pierced with a sense of sin is a sweet sacrifice to God. There is no offering more agreeable to God, and more delightful to offer, than a burning heart. Just as the flame came down from heaven and kindled the sacrifice, so the fire of the Spirit kindles our heart, and makes it go up to God.

A priest *in offering up praise*. One part of the priest's duty was to burn incense upon the golden altar. The golden altar represents Jesus; the incense, our prayers and praises. These, when put upon the golden altar rise sweetly up to heaven. Other prayers and praises never rise from the ground, but these mount up to heaven.

Dear friends, has this change passed upon you? By this you may know whether you are truly washed. These two cannot be separated. He hath washed us, and made us kings and priests.

Are you still the slave of sin, led captive by Satan at his will? Does he reign over you? Is his chain about your soul? Then you are not washed.

Are you no priest? Have you no access to God? Is your heart an altar without a sacrifice? No broken heart? No delight in giving all to God? Then you are yet in your sins.

Happy is that people whose God is the Lord. They and they only can say, He loved us, washed us, made us kings and priests to God and His Father. They have the broad seal of heaven upon their forehead. Oh, pray to be one of these.

*The song also invites us to consider,*

WHAT WE MUST DO FOR CHRIST.

I have done this for thee;
What hast thou done for Me?

'*To Him be glory.*' The saved soul longs to give glory to Christ. He looks back over all the way by which he has been led, and says from the bottom of his heart, *To Him be glory*. He looks to the love of Jesus – to his awakening, drawing, washing, renewing, making him a king and a priest. Ministers may have been used as instruments, but he looks far beyond these and says, *To Him be glory*. A true Christian will cast his crown nowhere but at the feet of Jesus. It was He that loved me, He that washed me. – *To Him be glory*.

*Try yourselves by this*. It is the clear mark of a hypocrite, that he is willing to cast his crown at the feet of a creature. Every jewel has its counterfeit, so there is a counterfeit conversion. Satan often changes people and makes them imagine they are converted. These will give the glory to man. They cast their crown at the feet of a fellow-worm and say, To him be glory. But one who is truly saved looks far above man, to Jesus, and says, 'To him be glory.' A man healed by the brazen serpent would never attribute it to the pole, or the man that held it. He would look steadily to the blazing sign that God had set up. A man saved by Jesus will say to all eternity, *To Him be glory* – 'Salvation to our God.' And when he comes into the New Jerusalem, he will not stop to look at the angels, nor fondly gaze on the redeemed, but will hasten to where Jesus sits, and fall down and worship and adore Him, casting his crown at His feet, and crying, 'Thou are worthy – Worthy is the Lamb that was slain' (Rev. 5:12).

To Him be '*dominion for ever*.' A saved soul gives himself away to Christ for ever. Before conversion a man loves to be his own master, to do what he will with his time, his money, his influence, his all. But when Jesus lays His hand on him, washes and renews him, then he says, 'I am the Lord's; I am not my own, but bought with a price. To Him be dominion for ever and ever.'

O Christians, come and give up your *all* to Christ – give up your heart to Him. Let His dominion be from sea to sea in your heart – from one corner to another. Is there any part of your heart where you do not wish Christ to reign? Then you have not seen Him, neither known Him. Give up your all to Him – your dearest friends. Say, they are not mine, but Christ's; and so you will part from them, not without a tear, but without losing your all. If there is anything you are unwilling Christ should have, then you are not His. *To Him be dominion.*

O, it is sweet, to have nothing our own, but to give up all to Christ – to be entirely His for ever and ever. Once you gave all to Satan. *Now* give all to Christ.

# 5

# John's Vision of Jesus in Glory –

One of the 'fragments that remain'

*'I John, who also am your brother, and companion in tribulation, and in the kingdom and patience of Jesus Christ, was in the isle that is called Patmos, for the word of God, and for the testimony of Jesus Christ. I was in the Spirit on the Lord's day, and heard behind me a great voice, as of a trumpet, saying, I am Alpha and Omega, the first and the last: and, What thou seest, write in a book, and send it unto the seven churches which are in Asia; unto Ephesus, and unto Smyrna, and unto Pergamos, and unto Thyatira, and unto Sardis, and unto Philadelphia, and unto Laodicea. And I turned to see the voice that spake with me. And, being turned, I saw seven golden candlesticks; and in the midst of the seven candlesticks one like unto the Son of man, clothed with a garment down to the foot, and girt about the paps with a golden girdle. His head and His hairs were white like wool, as white as snow; and His eyes were as a flame of fire; and His feet like unto fine brass, as if they burned in a furnace; and His voice as the sound of many waters. And He had in His right hand seven stars: and out of His mouth went a sharp two-edged sword:*

*and His countenance was as the sun shineth in his strength. And when I saw Him, I fell at His feet as dead. And He laid His right hand upon me, saying unto me, Fear not; I am the first and the last; I am He that liveth, and was dead; and behold, I am alive for evermore, Amen; and have the keys of hell and of death.'*
Revelation 1:9-18

John was keeping the Christian Sabbath in Patmos. Even though an exile, far from fellow-Christians, he was walking in the Spirit when God gave this blessed vision to him. Thus, my friends, even when away from the house of God, if you will seek to be in the Spirit, and to honour the Sabbath, God will make up for the want of ordinances.

Behold, what a glorious vision met the eye of John. One like unto the Son of Man, in the midst of the seven candlesticks – '*Like* unto the Son of Man' – not the same as when John leaned on His bosom – only like Him – far more glorious now. His garment was both kingly and priestly. His head and His hairs were white like wool, indicating eternal wisdom. His eyes were as a flame of fire, glowing with all searching knowledge. His feet were like burning brass, showing the dreadfulness of His tread, which burns and breaks. His voice was as the sound of many waters – so powerful and commanding. The sharp two-edged sword of the Word went out of His mouth. In His right hand were seven stars – His ministers hid in the hollow of His hand. His countenance was as the sun shineth in His strength, as it was on the Mount of Transfiguration – so bright that John could not look on Him. John had gone in and out with Jesus on the earth – had sat at meat with Him – had leaned on His bosom as a dear friend. But now how changed! He had seen Him on the mount, but this sight was far beyond that. He was now exalted and glorified, a name above every name, as, 'the Wonderful, the Counsellor, the mighty God, the everlasting Father, the Prince of Peace' (Isa. 9:6). Who could look on Him and live? '*I fell at His feet as dead.*'

But Jesus had the same heart in glory as He had on earth. 'He laid His right hand upon me' – that same hand which John had so often seen stretched out to heal, to rebuke fevers, to calm the troubled sea – the same which he had seen lifted up to bless. 'And He said, *Fear not.*' Often had the Saviour used these words on earth. 'Fear ye not, therefore: ye are of more value than many sparrows' (Matt. 10:31). 'Fear not, little flock; for it is your Father's good pleasure to give you the kingdom' (Luke 12:32). 'It is I, be not afraid.' (Matt. 14:27). But now they fell upon the ear of John as the sweet melody of many waters.

'I am the first and the last' – the same who spoke before; yet do not fear Me on that account. '*I am the living one – He that liveth* (John had written, 'In Him was life'), *and was dead; and, behold* (look on me)! *I am alive for evermore.*' He adds, '*Amen.*' Verily, verily – his constant expression to give weight, as if to say, This is all true.

*Doctrine.* A full view of Christ takes away all fear from the believing soul. To see Him as divine – a dead and a risen Saviour – is the great remedy to take away fear.

## I. The Previous Greatness of Christ Takes Away Fear.

He is the Alpha and Omega – the first and the last – and the living one. In Him dwelt all the fullness of the Godhead bodily. This takes away the fear of the believer. The threefold view of Christ as the eternally living one – as dead and as alive for evermore – is the only view which takes away fear.

To look at Christ as what He was before He came takes away fear. He was the Alpha and Omega, that is *All-wise*; the first and the last, who always *perfects what He begins. – He is All-wise* – Alpha and Omega. If a better way could have been devised, He would have known it. We may be sure it is the wisest way – most glorifying to God and safe to man. *He is all-perfecting.* Like the skilful workman who never lays hand on a thing without finishing – who holds it a dishonour to leave a work half-done, Christ never begins without finishing. He is the last as well as the first. Just as He completed creation in six days, and put the top-stone to the world, when He made all things new, so He is the first and last in redemption. It is a completed work – the work of the Son of God. A finished work: when it is begun it is as good as done. *He is the living one, and a sovereign Saviour.* He has all power in His hand – all life and all being. He is a willing Saviour – He came with His whole heart. Oh! believers this was the glorious Being that came to be your Saviour. He stretches out His hand to you, and says, 'Fear not.' When clouds and thick darkness compass Him about 'fear not.'

> Judge not the Lord by feeble sense,
> But trust Him for His grace;
> Behind a frowning providence
> He hides a smiling face.

Meditate on the greatness of Christ's original – of what He was before the world began, and say, I must be safe, for He undertook for me, who is all-wise, all-perfecting, and almighty.

Unbelievers, fear much – yea, tremble. When a mean servant stands at your door, you may say it is on a mean message. But when it is the king's son to whom you have denied admittance, you may well begin to tremble. You thought it was a man like yourselves, or a poor afflicted prophet; but behold, I tear away the veil, and He stands out the King in His beauty, 'Kiss the Son, lest He be angry, and ye perish from the way, when His wrath is kindled but a little' (Ps. 2:12).

## II. To Look at Jesus as Dead Takes away the Believer's Fear.

When John looked on those eyes of flame, piercing the deepest recesses of His bosom, as lightning pierces the darkest caverns – when he gazed on the pure white hairs of the Saviour, showing wisdom and holiness – when he saw those feet like burning brass, hot and strong to treat sinners under feet – then he fell as if dead. His beauty was turned into corruption. But Jesus says, '*Fear not, I was dead.*' I, the Alpha and Omega, the first and the last, and the living one – '*I was dead.*' I became man – veiled my glory in flesh, and died in the stead of guilty sinners. '*I was dead.*' Ah! my friends, this is the truth which gives peace to the anxious breast. This is balm for the sick. This is the argument by which the believer shuts out a thousand doubts and a thousand fears. Jesus speaks of it in glory – '*I was dead.*' He tells it to admiring angels, shows the marks of His wounds in His glorified body, and says, '*I was dead.*' Above all, He loves still to whisper it to the heart of a poor downcast believer. 'Fear not,' thou shalt never die. There is no wrath lying on you, for '*I was dead.*' Still more does He love to tell it to the believer at

His table, when He says, 'This is My body broken for you.' He points to the bread and wine – '*I was dead.*'

Unbelievers, there must be some dreadful cloud of wrath hanging over you, if this word be true – '*I was dead.*' If so great and wonderful a Being as the eternal Son of God became man and died, that a few poor worms of the earth believing in Him might not die eternally, then surely there is something in your case which you never thought of – some disease about you which is infinitely dreadful – there must be a hell beneath you infinitely deep. Ah! trifle not another hour. Jesus says, '*I was dead.*'

## III. To Look at Christ as Alive for Evermore, Takes Away the Believer's Fear.

It was a sight of His glorified body that made John fall down like one dead: it was so pure, and wonderful, and glorious. But now that Christ has told him of His death, He bids him look up and see His glory. 'Behold, I who was dead *am live for evermore.*'

Believers, this is your Saviour. Soon you shall see Him as He is. Till then, '*Fear not.*' Your Advocate is alive for evermore. He reigns for ever for His Church and people. All that divine wisdom is *for us*, His eyes are for us – His feet to tread down His and our enemies. He walks in the midst of the seven golden candlesticks, and holds the stars in His right hand. There is no hiding of His glory now – no hiding of His power. He lives for us – no evil can befall us – '*Fear not.*'

'Follow Jesus'
Matt. 9:9-13

Matthew was sitting at the receipt of custom when Jesus passed by. He was lying in his blood, when Jesus said, 'Live.' (reference to Ezekiel 16:6). How wonderful is the grace of the Lord Jesus. Some of you may be living in an evil calling, or in your sins. Look up, the Lord Jesus this night may turn His eye upon you.

*A simple word is blessed* – 'FOLLOW ME.' No argument. It is probable he had heard of Christ, heard Him preach, seen the preceding miracle; still he was at his old trade, till Jesus said, '*Follow* Me.' A little word reached his heart. We often make great mistakes – often make used of long arguments to bring people to Christ. Often we make use of long high-sounding words, and expect them to be blessed; whereas it is the simple exhibition of Christ that is carried home by the Spirit. If we could only set before you Him who is love embodied, and if the Spirit but breathe on the word, these little words 'Follow Jesus,' would break your soul away from all the world to follow Him. Speak for Christ. One little word may be blessed. 'Follow Jesus,' may win a soul.

*The soul that has once seen the loveliness of Christ, leaves all for Him.*

I doubt not Jesus gave Matthew a glimpse of His excellency. He felt the savour of Divine Love. He saw the gold – the pearl. What is all the world to him now? He cares not for its gains, its pleasure, its reproaches. In Christ he sees what is sweeter than all.

So *you*, if you have got a glimpse, you will not commune with flesh and blood. You will bid farewell to all. Farewell, gains of sin – pleasures of sin: in Christ I see a sweeter pleasure – a richer pearl.

Matthew *made a great feast*, and brought publicans. When he found that Jesus was so precious to a publican, he went and gathered all his fellow-sinners to meet with Jesus. It is probable he said within himself, 'I have often enticed them to sin; many a feast I have made; we have eaten and drunk together; now let me try and bring them to Jesus.'

You who have been called by Christ, can you do nothing to bring others to Him? You know that it is possible for such to be *saved*. You may have helped them in sin. Can you not *now* bring them to meet with Jesus? How many contrivances you might fall upon, if you had the compassion of Jesus.

Oh that Christians had more mercy, more of the bowels of Paul – of the spirit of Christ!

# 6

# Two Communion Addresses

## I.

*'And the very God of peace sanctify you wholly; and I pray God
your whole spirit and soul and body be preserved blameless unto
the coming of our Lord Jesus Christ.'*
1 Thessalonians 5:23

If there is any meaning in your sitting down at that table, and partaking of that bread and wine, then God is to you the 'very God of peace.' Once He was to you the God of vengeance, but now He is the very God of peace.

You can look back on a time when you lived under the wrath of the great God that made you. God was angry with you every day. You were altogether born in sin. Your heart was altogether depraved. You heaped up wrath against the day of wrath. Oh, do you not wonder that you are not in hell!

But you have fled to the bleeding Lamb, guilty and perishing. You have taken shelter in His wounds. You have this day openly accepted Him. Oh, if this be true, then God is the very God of peace to you. If I could this day go up into heaven, and open the books, and look into the records of the world, I would find your sins all blotted out, as a thick cloud; I would look up in the face of God and see Him smiling over you, saying, Thy sins and thine iniquities will I remember no more.

Dearly beloved and longed for, my joy and crown, rejoice evermore, for the God of vengeance is to you the very God of peace.

If, then, you have truly joined yourself to Christ at His table, this the affectionate prayer of my heart concerning you.

### 'THAT THE VERY GOD OF PEACE WOULD SANCTIFY YOU WHOLLY.'

My friends, the very use of being joined to Christ is to be made holy.

1. It is for this end Christ died. He died, not merely to redeem you from hell, but to bring you back to the image of His Father; to make you holy and happy.

2. It is for this very end the Holy Ghost is given. He dwells in your heart for no other end but to make you holy.

3. It is for this very end that the Gospel is preached Sabbath after Sabbath, that you may grow in holiness, in answer to the prayer of Christ, 'Sanctify them through Thy truth; Thy word is truth' (John 17:17).

4. It is for this very end that Sacraments are given, that you may thereby be strengthened to cleave to Christ, to overcome the world, and to live above it while in it.

If you are not made holy, then it is in vain for you that the Sacrament is spread – in vain the word is preached – in vain the Holy Ghost is given – in vain Christ died.

If you are not made holy, tell me not of your faith in Jesus, of your joy in the Word, of your delight in Sacraments. If you are not made holy thereby, it is all a lie. 'Be not deceived; he that doeth righteousness is righteous.' 'If ye love Me, keep My commandments.'

Do any among you ask, *How much holiness?* I answer, *Wholly.* If you have truly joined yourself to Christ, you will never aim at less than complete holiness. It is told of a true child of God, that, in his agonising struggles after holiness, he would often lie upon the ground and cry, 'Lord, give me up to sickness, give me up to suffering, give me up to death, but give me not up to any sin.' If you have indeed joined yourself to Christ, you will have the same desire after universal holiness. 'Let not any iniquity have dominion over me.' 'Quicken Thou me in Thy way.'

Blessed be God, it will be so with all of you who are joined to the Lord. Just as in the body, the heart doth send the healthful stream of blood to give life and energy to every limb and member of the body, so that even the minutest and weakest parts are kept full of life by the ever-circulating blood, – just as in the tree, the sap ascends up through the trunk, and spreads through the branches into the minutest fibres of every leaf, giving life and greenness to all, – so will it be in your hearts, ye members of Christ's body, ye precious branches of the true Vine. If ye be truly joined to Christ, the Holy Spirit will flow into every faculty of your soul – every faculty will become a little chamber to Jehovah's praise.

### 1. I PRAY GOD YOUR AFFECTIONS MAY BE SANCTIFIED.

Take heed what you love. Love what Jesus loved. Love not the world, neither the things that are in the world. Set your affection on things above, not on things on the earth. Love not money; it is the root of all evil. Love Jesus. Forgiven much, love much. Love God; He is worthy of all the love. Love the brethren; make them the chosen friends of your soul.

### 2. I PRAY GOD YOUR UNDERSTANDING MAY BE SANCTIFIED.

A sanctified understanding is worth all the godless wisdom of earth and of hell. O! what fools the wisest of natural men appear when they die. Remember that, if you be joined to Christ, you will receive the 'spirit of power, and of love, and of a sound mind.'

### 3. I PRAY GOD YOUR HABITS MAY BE SANCTIFIED.

*Live in secret prayer.* – Oh, if you would every morning enter into the secret of God's presence, how your face would shine throughout the day! Often through the day let your heart rise up to Him with secret boundings; and at night close all with Him. How sweet to work all the day in His favour, and lie down at night under His smile.

*Live in family prayer.* – My dear friends, you are not Christians if you have no family prayer. You may come to the house of God, and you may sit down at Sacraments, but, if ye be heads of families, and yet refuse to kneel with them before the God of families, you are not Christians – you are not the children of Abraham. This did not Abraham. *Begin to-night.* Say, 'As for me and my house, we will serve the LORD' (Josh. 24:15).

*Read the Bible.* – If ye be led by the Spirit, ye will love the Bible. You will say, Oh, 'How love I Thy law, it is my meditation all the day.' Be determined to learn something new out of the Bible every day. 'I have lost a world of time,' said one, when dying. 'If I had another year to live, I would spend it in reading David's Psalms and Paul's Epistles.' Oh, be wiser in your Bibles than in the newspaper. What good will all that ever you read in the newspaper do when you are dying? Alas! for my beloved land, when the newspaper drives the Bible from its place by the cottage fire.

## 4. I Pray God Your Body May be Sanctified.

If you be joined to Christ, your body will become the temple of the Holy Ghost. Be holy in body, dear Christians. Present your bodies a living sacrifice, holy and acceptable to the Lord. Christ is also the Saviour of the body. *May your eyes*, that were once full of adultery, become pure, shining only with looks of faith and Christ-like tenderness. *May your feet*, that once carried you to the haunts of godless pleasure, be shod with the preparation of the gospel of peace. May they be ever beautiful, because they carry the message of peace. *May your hands*, that once handled unlawful things, now minister to the poor, the widow, and the orphan. May they wash the saint's feet. *Your belly* was once your god, and you glorified in your shame; now joined to Christ, you will flee intemperance. Remember you cannot drink the cup of the Lord and the cup of devils. Above all, dearly beloved, abstain from fleshy lusts, which war against the soul. 'And such were some of you; but ye are washed.' Remember, then, ye are now the members of Christ. 'Shall I then take the members of Christ, and make them the members of an harlot? God forbid' (1 Cor. 6:15).

Oh, dear brethren, give Christ your body to keep, and He will keep it against that day.

*How long?* Till the coming of the Lord Jesus. This is my prayer for you, that you may be kept till that day. That Great Day is surely at hand now. For yourselves know that the Day of the Lord cometh as a thief in the night. It is long, long since he said, I come quickly.

Many of you have times of trouble at hand. Days of darkness are near to some of you. Days of temptation are coming to some of you – opportunities to sin in ways you never thought of. Yet fear not, dear brethren, if you have joined yourselves to Christ. I pray that you may be preserved blameless unto the coming of the Lord Jesus.

## God is Faithful, Who Also Will Do It.

My friends, if we had to rely on you for your future walk in the world we would despair. I bless and praise my God that He has touched the hearts of many of you: and yet *what are you in yourselves?* Broken reeds – a withered leaf – helpless babes.

*What are your enemies?* – Look around you. The world lying in wickedness is against you. 'I send you forth as sheep in the midst of wolves' (Matt. 10:16). O, look down to hell; there are crafty devils – mighty spirits of evil, all, all against you. How, then, should we hope such things from you? Ah! God is faithful, who also will do it. I lean my back upon the Rock of Ages, and I feel there is enough in Him to enable me to stand against all the world. If you are joined to Christ, God is for you; God the Father is a shield all around you; God the Holy Ghost is within you. If you are joined to Christ, then God is a Covenant God to you.

You remember when Elisha and his servant were in Dothan, and a great host of enemies compassed them in, the young man cried, Alas, my master, how shall we do? And Elisha answered, Fear not, for they that be with us, are more than they that be with them. 'And Elisha prayed, and said, "LORD, I pray thee, open his eyes that he may see." And the LORD opened the eyes of the young man, and he saw, and behold, the mountain was full of horses and chariots of fire round about Elisha' (2 Kings 6:15-17).

Dear brethren, believe what you do not see. Live by faith in a Covenant-keeping God. 'God is faithful, who also will do it.'

## II.

*'Confirming the souls of the disciples, and exhorting them to continue in the faith, and that we must through much tribulation enter into the kingdom of God'.*
Acts 14:22

I trust a goodly number of you, dear brethren, have been this day added to the church of such as shall be saved. Many of you, I trust, in taking that bread and wine into your hands, could joyfully say, 'I know that my Redeemer liveth. This is my beloved, and this is my friend.' Many of you I trust, fixed your eyes and your hearts on the holy, harmless, undefiled High Priest, and offered your souls and bodies through Him. To all such I would now say

### CONTINUE IN THE FAITH.
*This is the way to have abiding peace.* Some of you to-day came labouring and heavy laden, but the veil was taken

away, and Jesus in all His fullness and beauty was revealed, bearing our sins in His own body on the tree. Your burden fell, and a divine peace pervaded your soul. 'Oh! that I could feel this peace for ever!' is the language of your heart. Continue in the faith. Run, looking unto Jesus. Keep the eye of your faith fixed on Him. Some seem to think that we are to find peace at first by looking to Christ, and afterwards by seeing the life of God advancing in your own soul. No, beloved, you must be justified on your dying-bed, in the same way as at your first Lord's table. You must be righteous altogether in another. Keep the eye fixed on Jesus. Clear away all dimness. Look ever on the sinless One, in whom alone you stand.

*This is the way to become holy.* – Continue in the faith. It is the presence of God with the soul that sanctifies. The Lord God is a sun and shield; but it is only when we abide in Christ that we are brought nigh. Keep yourselves in the love of God. He loves you too well to give you up to sin.

It is the indwelling of the Holy Spirit that sanctifies; but He dwells only in the heart that is in Jesus. Some of you are panting after God's commandments, anxious to know how you shall be made holy. This is the way – continue in the faith.

*This is the way to pass through afflictions.* – When a man's eye is closed on Christ and the eternal world, he cannot stand the shock of afflictions; but if his eyes clearly see Jesus, you may take away houses and lands, his dearest earthly possessions, his loved ones, still his chief treasure is untouched.

*This is the way to die in peace* – It is a solemn thing to die, – to leave all that we have seen, and tasted, and handled. One thing only will support – looking unto Jesus. If we have a real sight of Jesus standing between us and the Father – our Righteousness – our High Priest, who bore our sins, and cleanses us still, – this will fill our hearts with heavenly peace. Death has no terrors for a believing soul. One dear believer has entered into her rest since last Sabbath day. In the full assurance of faith she raised her dying hand and softly said, 'If it were His will, I would like to depart this night and be with Christ.'

## There is a 'Need Be' for Much Tribulation

We naturally shrink from pain. Many would like to go round; no, we must go through. Many would be willing to have a little; but no, we must through much tribulation enter the kingdom.

There are three streams of trouble peculiar to believers.

*Persecution.* – Let us go without the camp bearing His reproach – take up our cross daily. This is what Moses had to bear, and Lot, and all God's children, – trials of cruel mockings and scourgings.

*Temptations.* – There is a 'need be' for this also. Satan is a fearful enemy. Before conversion, we know little of him. Those who are determined to win glory, will feel his fiery darts. There is a design on Satan's part. He will not suffer us to go quietly into the kingdom. And on God's part, too, He wants us to know what we are saved from.

*Concern for unconverted souls.* – This is one of the deep afflictions of a child of God. He is afflicted for unconverted kindred. It may be father, mother, sister, brother, friend; the wife of his bosom, or the children of his love; unconverted neighbours, an unbelieving world. This is a sorrow he must carry with him to the grave.

O dear friends, make up your minds to carry the cross daily. Fore-warned is to be fore-armed. All God's children go through these tribulations. But Christ will be with us in all until we

### Enter into the Kingdom of God.

Soon we shall have no more sorrow. It is a dark cloud, – oh, how dark at times! But it is passing, all is light beyond. We 'shall obtain joy and gladness, and sorrow and sighing shall flee away' (Isa. 35:10).

We shall sin no more – fight no more with corruptions. The night is far spent; the day is at hand.

# 7

# THE CRY FOR REVIVAL

*'Wilt Thou not revive us again, that Thy people may rejoice in Thee.'*
Psalm 85:6

I t is interesting to notice the *time when this prayer was offered*. It was a time of mercy. 'Lord, Thou has been favourable unto Thy land' (Ps. 85:1). It was a time when God had led many to the knowledge of Christ, and covered many sins. 'Thou hast forgiven the iniquity of Thy people.' It was now they began to feel their need of another visit of mercy – 'Wilt Thou not revive us again?'

*The thing prayed for*. 'Revive us again,' or literally, return and make us live anew. It is the prayer of those who have received some life, but feel their need of more. They had been made alive by the Holy Spirit. They felt the sweetness and excellence of this new, hidden, divine life. They pant for more – 'Wilt Thou not revive us again?'

*The argument presented.* 'That Thy people may rejoice in Thee.' They plead with God to do this for the sake of His people; that their joy may be full; and that it may be in the Lord – in the Lord their Righteousness – in the Lord their strength.

## I. WHEN THIS PRAYER IS NEEDED.

1. In a time of *Backsliding*. There are times when, like Ephesus, many of God's children lose their first love. Iniquity abounds, and the love of many waxes cold. *Believers* lose their close and tender walking with *God*. They lose their close and near communion with *God*. They go out of the holiest, and pray at a distance with a curtain between. They lose their fervency, sweetness, and fullness in secret prayer. They do not pour out their hearts to God.

They have lost their clear discovery of *Christ*. They see Him but dimly. They have lost the sight of His beauty – the savour of His good ointment – the hold of His garment. They seek Him, but find Him not. They cannot stir up the heart to lay hold on Christ.

The *Spirit* dwells scantily in their soul. The living water seems almost dried up within them. The soul is dry and barren. Corruptions are strong: grace is very weak.

*Love to the brethren fades.* United prayer is forsaken. The little assembly no more appears beautiful. Compassion for the unconverted is low and cold. Sin is unrebuked though committed under their eye. Christ is not confessed before men. Perhaps the soul falls into sin, and is afraid to return; it stays far off from God, and lodges in the wilderness.

Ah! this is the case, I fear, with many. It is a fearfully dangerous time. Nothing but a visit of the Free Spirit to your soul can persuade you to return. Is it not a time for this prayer – 'Wilt Thou not revive us again?'

2. A time of *Temptation*. The soul of a believer needs grace every moment. 'By the grace of God I am what I *am*.' But there are times when he needs more grace than at other times. Just as the body continually needs food; but there are times when it needs food more than at others – times of great bodily exertion, when all the powers are to be put forth.

Sometimes the soul of a believer is exposed to *hot persecution*. Reproach breaks the heart; or it beats like a scorching sun upon the head. 'For my love they are my adversaries' (Ps. 109:4). Sometimes they are God's children who reproach us, and this is still harder to bear. The soul is ready to fret or sink under it.

Sometimes it is *flattery* that tempts the soul. The world speaks well of us, and we are tempted to pride and vanity. This is still worse to bear.

Sometimes *Satan strives within us*, by stirring up fearful corruptions, till there is tempest within. Oh, is there a tempted soul here? Jesus prays for thee. Pray for thyself. You need more peace. Nothing but the oil of the Spirit will feed the fire of grace when Satan is casting water on it. Send up this cry, 'Wilt Thou not revive us again?'

3. A time of *Concern*. 'Ask ye of the LORD rain in the time of the latter rain' (Zech. 10:1). When God begins a time of concern in a place – when the dew is beginning to fall – *then* is the time to pray, Lord stay not Thine hand – give us a full shower – leave not one dry. 'Wilt Thou not revive us again?'

## II. WHO NEED THIS REVIVAL.

*1. Ministers need it.* Ministers are naturally hard-hearted and unbelieving as other men (Mark 16:14), so that Christ has often to upbraid them. Their faith is all from above. They must receive from God all that they give. In order to speak the truth with power, they need a personal grasp of it. It is impossible to speak with power from mere head knowledge, or even from past experience. If we would speak with energy, it must be from present feeling of the truth as it is in Jesus. We cannot speak of the hidden manna unless we have the taste of it in our mouth. We cannot speak of the living water unless it be springing up within us. Like John the Baptist, we must see Jesus coming, and say 'Behold the Lamb of God.' We must speak with Christ in our eye, as Stephen did. 'I see Jesus standing on the right hand of God.' We must speak from present sense of pardon and access to God, or our words will be cold and lifeless. But how can we do this if we be not quickened from above? Ministers are far more exposed to be cast down than other men; they are standard-bearers, and Satan loves when a standard-bearer fainteth, O, what need of full supplies out of Christ's fullness! Pray, beloved, that it may be so. 'Wilt Thou not revive us again?'

*2. God's children need it.* The divine life is all from above. They have no life till they come to Christ. 'Except ye eat the flesh of the Son of Man, and drink His blood, ye have no life in you' (John 6:53). Now this life is maintained by union to Christ, and by getting fresh supplies every moment out of His fullness. 'He that eateth My flesh and drinketh My blood dwelleth in Me, and I in Him.' (John 6:56). In some believers this life is maintained by a constant inflowing of the Holy Spirit – 'I will water it every moment' – like the constant supply which the branch receives from the vine. These are the happiest and most even Christians. Others have flood-tides of the Spirit carrying them higher and higher. Sometimes they get more in a day than for months before. In the one of these grace is like a river; in the other, it is like the shower coming down in its season. Still, in both there is need of revival. The natural heart in all is prone to wither. Like a garden in summer, it dries up unless watered. The soul grows faint and weary in well-doing. Grace is not natural to the heart. The old heart is always for dying and fading. So the child of God needs to be continually looking out, like Elijah's servant, for the little cloud over the sea. You need to be constantly pressing near to the Fountain of living waters; yea, lying down at the well-head of salvation, and drinking the living water. 'Wilt Thou not revive us again?'

3. *Those that were awakened, and have gone back, need it.* A drop fell from heaven upon their heart. They trembled, wept, prayed. But the shower passed by, and the rocky heart ceased to tremble. The eye again closed in slumber; the lips forgot to pray. Ah, how common and sad is this case! The King of Zion lifted up his voice in this place and cried. Some that were in their graves heard His voice, and began to live. But this passed by, and now they sink back again into the grave of a dead soul. Ah! this is the fearful state! To go back to death, to love death, and wrong your own soul. What can save such a one, but another call from Jesus? 'Awake, thou that sleepest, and arise from the dead, and Christ shall give thee light.' For your sake most of all I pray, 'Wilt Thou not revive us again?'

4. *Barren Fig-trees need it.* Some of you have been planted in this vineyard. You have enjoyed sun and shower. You have passed through all this time of awakening without being moved. You are still dead, barren, unconverted, fruitless. Ah! there is for you no hope but in this prayer. Ordinary times will not move you. Your heart is harder than that of other men. What need have you to pray for a deep, pure, effectual work of God, and that you may not be passed by. Many of you would stand the shock much better now. You have grown experienced in resisting God, and quenching this Spirit. Oh, pray for a time that will remove mountains. None but the Almighty Spirit can touch your hard heart. 'Who art thou, O great mountain? before Zerubbabel thou shalt become a plain.' 'Wilt Thou not revive us again; that Thy people may rejoice in Thee?'

## III.   FROM WHOM REVIVAL COMES.

It is *God* who must revive us again. It is not a human work. It is all divine. If you look to men to do it, you will only get that curse in Jeremiah 17, 'Cursed be the man that trusteth in man, and maketh flesh his arm.'

1. The Lord has all the means in His hands. The Son of Man holds the seven stars in His right hand. These stars are ministers. He lifts them up, or lets them down, at His sovereign will. He gives them all their light, or He takes it away. He holds them up and lets them shine clearly, or He hides them in the hollow of His hand, as it seemeth good in His sight. Sometimes He lets them shine on one district of a country, sometimes on another. They only shine to lead to Him. The star that leads away from Him is a wandering star, and Christ will cast it into the blackness

of darkness for ever. We should pray to Christ to make His ministers shine on us.

2. The Lord has the fullness of the Spirit given to Him. The Father has entrusted the whole work of redemption into the hands of Jesus, and so the Spirit is given to Him. 'As the Father hath life in Himself, and quickeneth whom He will, so hath He given to the Son to have life in Himself, and to quicken whom He will.'

It is He who keeps all His own children alive from day to day. He is the Fountain of living waters, and His children lie beside the still waters, and drink every moment eternal life from Him.

It is He that pours down the Spirit in His sovereignty on those that never knew Him. 'I will pour upon the house of David, and upon the inhabitants of Jerusalem, the Spirit of grace and of supplications' (Zech. 12:10). Truly the whole work from beginning to end is His.

Every means will be in vain until He pours the Spirit down (Isa. 32:13): 'Upon the land of My people shall come up thorns and briers,' *until* the Spirit be poured upon us from on high. We may preach publicly, and from house to house; we may teach the young, and warn the old, but all will be in vain, *until* the Spirit be poured upon us from on high, briers and thorns shall grow. Our vineyard shall be like the garden of the sluggard. We need that Christ should awake; that He should make bare His arm as in the days of old; that He should shed down the Spirit abundantly.

3. *The children of God should plead with Him.* Put your finger on the promise, and plead, 'When the poor and needy seek water, and there is none, I the LORD will hear them.' (Isa. 41:17). Tell Him you are poor and needy.

Spread out your wants before Him. Take your emptiness to His fullness. There is an infinite supply with Him for everything you need, at the very moment you need it.

4.   Ungodly men, you are saying, there is no promise to us. But there is, if you will receive it. Psalms 68:18: 'Thou hast ascended on high; Thou hast led captivity captive; Thou hast received gifts from men; yea; for the rebellious also.' Are you a rebel? Go and tell Him so. Oh, if you are willing to be justified by Him, and to get your rebel heart changed, go and ask Him, and He will give you living water. Proverbs 1:23: 'Turn you at My reproof; behold I will pour out My Spirit unto you.' Go and tell Him you are a 'simple one, a scorner.' Ask Him to do what He has promised in Ezekiel 34:26: 'I will make them and the places round about My hill, a blessing: and I will cause the shower to come down in his season; there shall be showers of blessing.' Now, you cannot say you belong to Zion-hill, but you can say you are in the places round about this hill. Oh cry, 'Wilt Thou not revive us again?'

## IV. THE EFFECTS OF A REVIVAL.

*1.   The Lord's children rejoice in Him.* They rejoice in Christ Jesus. The purest joy in the world is joy in Christ Jesus. When the Spirit is poured down, His people get very near and clear views of the Lord Jesus. They eat His flesh and drink His blood. They come to a personal cleaving to the Lord. They taste that the Lord is gracious. His blood and righteousness appear infinitely perfect, full, and free to their soul. They sit under His shadow with great delight. They rest in the clefts of the rock. Their defence is the munitions of rocks. They lean on the beloved. They find infinite strength in Him for the use of their soul – grace for grace – all they can need in any house of trial and suffering to the very end.

They go by Him to the Father. 'We joy in God through our Lord Jesus Christ.' We find a portion there – a shield, and exceeding great reward. This gives joy unspeakable and full of glory.

Now, God loves to see His children happy in Himself. He loves to see all our springs in Him. Take and plead that. Oh, you would pray after a different manner if God were to pour water on the thirsty. You would tell Him all, open to Him all sorrows, joys, cares, comforts. All would be told to Him.

2. *Many flock to Christ.* 'Who are these that fly like a cloud, and like doves to their windows?' 'To Him shall the gathering of the people be.' Just as all the creatures came into the ark, so poor sinners run in such a time. Laying aside their garments (Mark 10:50), their jealousies, they flee together into the ark Jesus. Oh, there is not a lovelier sight in all this world.

*Souls are saved.* 'Is this not a brand plucked out of the fire?' There is therefore now no condemnation to them which are in Christ Jesus.' They are passed from death unto life.

*It is glorifying to God.* 'He that receives Christ, sets to his seal that God is true.' He confesses the holiness of God, His love and grace. His mouth is filled with praise. 'Bless the Lord O my soul!' He begins to long for the image of God, to confess Him before men, to walk in His ways. It gives joy in heaven, and joy on earth. Oh, pray for such a time.

*There is an awakening again of those who have gone back.* If we have not a time of the outpouring of the Spirit, many who once sought Christ, but have gone back, will perish in a dreadful manner; for they generally turn worse than before. Sometimes they scoff and make a jest of all. Satan is all the worse that he was once an angel. So they become all the more wicked who have gone back. They generally go deeper into the mire of sin. But if God graciously pours down His Spirit, the hardened heart will melt. Pray for this.

*There is an awakening of fresh sinners.* It is a sad state of things when sinners are bold in sin; when multitudes can openly break the Sabbath, and openly frequent the tavern. It is an awful sign when sinners can live in sin, and yet sit unmoved under the preaching of the Word, cast off fear and restrain prayer before God. But if the Lord were pleased to revive us again, this state of things would be changed.

I am sure it would be a lovelier sight to see you going up in company to the house of prayer, than thronging to the tavern, or to the haunts of sin or shame, that will bring down eternal ruin on your poor soul. It would be sweeter to hear the cry of prayer in your closets, than to hear the sound of oaths and profane jesting, and your hard speeches and reproaches of God's children. Sweeter far to see your hearts panting after Christ, His pardon, His holiness, His glory, than to see them burning after the world and its vain idols.

Oh, Lift up your hearts to the Lord for such a time. Plead earnestly the promise, 'I will pour my Spirit upon all flesh.' Then this wilderness will become a fruitful field, and its name be, JEHOVAH-SHAMMAH – The LORD is there.

*Excerpt from 'From the Preacher's Heart'*
*by R.M. McCheyne ...*

# CHRIST'S LOVE TO THE CHURCH

*Husbands, love your wives, even as Christ also loved the church, and gave himself for it; that he might sanctify and cleanse it with the washing of water by the word, that he might present it to himself a glorious church, not having spot, or wrinkle, or any such thing; but that it should be holy and without blemish* (Eph. 5:25-27).

In this passage the apostle, under the guidance of the Spirit, is teaching wives and husbands their duties to one another. To the wives he enjoins submission – a loving yielding to their husbands in all lawful things; to the husbands, love; and he puts before them the highest of all patterns – Christ and His Church.

## 1. Christ's love to His Church

*The object of His love.*
The Church – all who are chosen, awakened, believing, justified, sanctified, glorified; all who are finally saved – all who shall stand with the Lamb, the hundred and forty and four thousand redeemed ones, all looked on as the bright company; the Church – all who are awakened and brought to Christ, all who shall sit down at the marriage supper.

I believe Jesus had compassion for the whole world. He is not willing that any should perish. He willeth all men to be saved. He shed tears over those who will finally perish.

Still, the peculiar object of His love was the Church. He loved the Church. On them His eye rested with peculiar tenderness before the world was. He would often say: These shall yet sit with me on my throne; or, as he read over their names in His book of life, he would say: These shall yet walk with me in white. When they lived in sin, His eye was upon them. He would not let them die, and drop into hell: 'I have much people in this city.' I have no doubt, brethren, Christ is marking some of you, that are now Christless, for His own. When they came to Christ, He let out His love toward them on the land where they dwelt – a delightsome land. His eye rests on the houses of this town, where His jewels live. Christ loves some streets far better than others – some spots of earth are far dearer to Him than others.

Christ loved His Church. Just as a husband at sea loves the spot where His dear wife dwells, so does the Lord Jesus: 'I have graven thee upon the palms of my hands' (Isaiah 49:16). He loves some in one house far more than others. There are some apartments dear to Christ – where He is often present – where His hands are often on the door: 'Open to me, my love.'

*The state of the Church when first loved.*
1. They were *all under the curse of God* – under condemnation – exposed to the just wrath of God – deserving nothing but wrath; for 'He gave himself for it'. The Church had no dowry to attract the love of Jesus, except her wrath and curse.

2. *Impure.* For he had to 'sanctify and cleanse it'; unholy within – opposed to God – no beauty in the eye of Jesus: I am black, spotted, and wrinkled.

3. *Nothing to draw the love of Christ.* Nothing that he could admire in them. He admires whatever is like His Father.

He had eternally gazed upon His Father, and was ravished with that beauty; but He saw none of this – not a feature – no beauty at all. Men love where they see something to draw esteem – Christ saw none.

4. *Everything to repel His love*: 'Polluted in thine own blood' – cast out – loathsome (Ezekiel 16); yet that was the time of His love. Black – uncomely: 'Thou hast loved me out of the pit of corruption.'

5. *Not from ignorance*. Men often love where they do not know the true character, and repent after. But not so Christ. He knew the weight of their sins – the depths of their wicked heart.

Nothing is more wonderful than the love of Christ. *Learn the freeness of the love of Christ*. It is unbought love. 'If a man would give all the substance of his house for love, it would be utterly contemned' (Song 8:7). He drew all His reasons from Himself: 'I knew that thou wast obstinate.' You have no cause to boast. He loved you, because he loved you – for nothing in you. O what a black soul wast thou, when Christ set his love upon thee!

*The greatness of that love*: 'He gave Himself.'
This is unparalleled love. Love is known by the sacrifice it will make. In a fit of love, Herod would have given away the half of his kingdom. If you will sacrifice nothing, you love not. Hereby we know that men love not Christ – they will sacrifice nothing for Him. They will not leave a lust – a game – a companion, for Christ. 'Greater love than this hath no man.' But Christ gave Himself. Consider what a

self. If he had created ten thousand millions of worlds, and given them away, it had been great love. Had He given a million of angels; but He gave the Lord of angels, the Creator of worlds. 'Lo, I come.' He gave the pearl of heaven. O what a self! – Jesus! – all loveliness!

*What he gave Himself to.*
He gave himself to be put in their place – to bear their wrath and curse, and to obey for them. We shall never know the greatness of this gift. He gave himself to bear the guilt of the Church. There cannot be a more fearful burden than guilt, even if there be no wrath. To the holy soul of Jesus, this was an awful burden. He was made sin: 'mine iniquities have taken hold upon me, so that I am not able to look up' (Psalm 40:12). 'For mine iniquities are gone over mine head: as a heavy burden, they are too heavy for me' (Psalm 38:4). He endured the cross, despising the shame. He laid His soul under their guilt – shame and spitting; silent like a lamb.

*To bear their wrath.* A happy soul shrinks from suffering. Ask one that has always been in the love of God, what for would he cast himself out of that love – bear as much wrath as He is bearing love – receive the lightning instead of the sunshine? Not for ten millions of worlds. Yet this did Jesus. He became a curse for us: Pour it out on me. See how He shrunk back from it in the garden. Yet He drank it.

'God commendeth his love to us, in that, while we were yet enemies, Christ died for us.' Pray to know the love of Christ. It is a great ocean, without bottom or shore.' ('It is as if a child could take the globe of earth and sea in his two short arms' – Samuel Rutherford.) In the broken bread you will see it set forth so that a child may understand: 'This is my body, broken for you.' 'This is my blood, shed for many.'

## 2. His purpose in time (verse 26)

Christ's work is not done with a soul when He has brought it to pardon – when He has washed it in His own blood. Oh, no! the better half of salvation remains – His great work of sanctification remains.

### *Who is the author?*
He that gave Himself for the Church – the Lamb that was slain. God having raised His Son Jesus, sent Him to bless you, in turning every one of you away from your inquiries. He is exalted by the right hand of God, and, having obtained the promise of the Father, sheds Him down. There is no hand can new-create the soul, but the hand that was pierced. Many look to a wrong quarter for sanctification. They take pardon from Christ, then lean on themselves – their promises, etc. – for holiness. Ah, no! you must take hold of the hand that was pierced – lean on the arm that was racked – lean on the Beloved coming up from the wilderness. You might as well hold up the sun on its journey as sanctify yourself. It needs divine power. There are three concerned in it. The Father – for this is His will; the Son – He is the Shepherd of all He saves; the Holy Ghost.

### *The means.*
'The Word.' I believe He could sanctify without the Word, as He created angels and Adam holy, and as He

84

sanctifies infants whose ear was never opened; but I believe in grown men He never will, but through the Word. When Jesus makes holy, it is by writing the Word in the heart: 'Sanctify them through thy truth.' When a mother nurses her child, she not only bears it in her arms, but holds it to her breast, and feeds it with the milk of her own breast; so does the Lord. He not only holds the soul, but feeds it with the milk of the Word. The words of the Bible are just the breathings of God's heart. He fills the heart with these, to make us like God. When you go much with a companion, and hear His words, you are gradually changed by them into His likeness; so when you go with Christ, and hear His words, you are sanctified. Oh, there are some whom I could tell to be Christ's, by their breathing the same sweet breath! Those of you that do not read your Bible cannot turn like God – you cannot be saved. You are unsaveable; you may turn like the devil, but you never will turn like God. Oh, believers, prize the Word!

3. *The certainty of it.*
Some are afraid they will never be holy: 'I shall fall under my sin.' You shall be made holy. It was for this Christ died. This was the grand object He had in view. This was what was in His eye – to build a holy Church out of a world of lost sinners; to pluck brands out of the fire, and make them trees of righteousness; to choose poor, black souls, and make them fair brothers and sisters round His throne. Christ will not lose this object.

Look up, then – be not afraid. He redeemed you to make you holy. Though you had a million of worlds opposing you, He will do it: 'He is faithful, who also will do it.'

### 3. His purpose in eternity – twofold

*Its perfection:* 'A glorious Church.'
At present believers are sadly imperfect. They have on the perfect righteousness that will be no brighter above; but they are not perfectly holy; they mourn over a body of sin – spots and wrinkles. Neither are they perfectly happy. Often crushed; waves go over them; like the moon waning. But they shall be perfectly glorious. Perfect in righteousness – white robes, washed in the blood of the Lamb. Perfect in holiness – filled with the Holy Spirit. Perfect in happiness – this shall be. It is all in the covenant.

*He will present it to Himself.*
He will be both father and bridegroom. He has bought the redeemed – He will give them away to Himself. The believer will have great nearness, he shall see the King in His beauty. Great intimacy – walk with Him, speak with Him. He shall have oneness with Him: 'All that I have is thine'.

*St Peter's, January, 1841 (Action Sermon)*

*Also available from Christian Focus ...*

Constrained by his Love

A New Biography
on
Robert Murray McCheyne

LJ Van Valen

ISBN 978-1-85792-793-1

# Constrained By His Love

## A New Biography
## of Robert Murray McCheyne

### L.L. VAN VALEN

Robert Murray McCheyne was born in 1813 and died in 1843. His life, was nothing short of extraordinary. Given the charge of St Peter's Church, Dundee at the age of 23, even his trial sermon was blessed, with two people being saved. The church saw astonishing growth, overflowing with 1,100 hearers.

He stands today as one of the outstanding preachers in the history of Scotland. His spirituality, and focus on the work of Christ was immediately apparent – with hostile crowds melting as they realised the sincerity of the man and the power of his message.

His life is a lesson to us all, that when we submit to our Sovereign Lord and His plan, He can and will use our bodies, no matter how weak, our gifts, no matter how limited and our lives, no matter how short.

*He was an outstanding man of God, and his life story, here told in fullest detail and with fullest sympathy, should on no account be missed.*

J. I. PACKER
Well known author & Board of Governors' Professor of Theology,
Regent College, Vancouver, Canada

"...a fine and fresh account of a great
and godly minister of the gospel."

Eric Alexander

# AWAKENING
## THE LIFE & MINISTRY OF
## ROBERT MURRAY MᶜCHEYNE

David Robertson

ISBN 978-1-84550-542-4

# Awakening

## *The Life & Ministry of*
## *Robert Murray McCheyne*

### DAVID ROBERTSON

'Was McCheyne for real?'; 'Was he just famous because he died so young?'; 'Does he have anything to teach us today?'

In this book, David Robertson, the present-day minister of McCheyne's church, St Peter's in Dundee, Scotland, seeks to answer these and other questions. Through the use of published sermons, private papers and historical material, this contemporary devotional biography traces McCheyne's life and influence from his upbringing, conversion and training for the ministry to the revival that occurred in St. Peter's in 1839 and his early death.

The contemporary relevance of McCheyne for today's church is demonstrated and the glory of God is seen in this wonderful story of what He can do with one 'consecrated sinner'.

*... a fine and fresh account of a great and godly minister of the gospel. David Robertson gives us new insight into McCheyne's personal life, and his preparation for preaching, his deep social concern and his absolute devotion to the glory of God as the ultimate motive of everything he did.*

ERIC ALEXANDER
Conference speaker and former minister
St George's Tron, Glasgow

ISBN 978-1-85792-258-5

# Mission of Discovery
## *The Beginnings of Modern Jewish Evangelism*
### Andrew Bonar and R.M. McCheyne

The journal of Bonar and McCheyne's Mission of inquiry, 1839. This epic chronicle has a fascination that stems from the attention to detail both men had for what they saw. It is part travel book, adventure story, and social history.

This is an absorbing story of the scattered Jewish people of the mid 19th century and the problems of travel in politically unstable situations. As a result of this journey the first Church of Scotland missionary to the Jews was sent to Hungary in 1841.

THE
SEVEN
CHURCHES
OF ASIA

ROBERT
MURRAY MᶜCHEYNE

ISBN 978-0-90673-151-2

# The Seven Churches of Asia
## *The Beginnings of Modern Jewish Evangelism*
### Robert Murray McCheyne

From one of Scotland's greatest preachers, Robert Murray McCheyne, we have this fascinating collection of sermons that were preached during a period of great revival in Scotland. With seven sermons, one on each of the churches in Ephesus, Smyrna, Pergamos, Thyatira, Sardis, Philadelphia and Laodicea, we are offered valuable insights into the distinctives of these early church situations. They give the reader some idea of McCheyne's great burden to see men and women coming to know Christ for themselves.

Dr Baxter wrote of McCheyne 'the chief thing about him was the unction from the Holy Spirit ... at times he was awakening ... at other times he was melting and moving as he dwelt on the great theme of redeeming love.'

His epitaph describes him as a man who 'was honoured by his Lord to draw many wanderers out of darkness into the path of life.'

*These samples of McCheyne's work are utterly Christ-centred. He incessantly pointed listeners, and now readers also, to Christ for eternal life and for sanctified living ... This volume is therefore highly recommended to all, particularly as a devotional aid, and also to preachers as an abiding monument and yardstick of God-glorifying proclamation.*

Tim J. R. Trumper
Seventh Reformed Church, Grand Rapids, Michigan

# Christian Focus Publications

Our mission statement –

STAYING FAITHFUL

In dependence upon God we seek to impact the world through literature faithful to His infallible Word, the Bible. Our aim is to ensure that the Lord Jesus Christ is presented as the only hope to obtain forgiveness of sin, live a useful life and look forward to heaven with Him.

Our books are published in four imprints:

### CHRISTIAN
## FOCUS

Popular works including biographies, commentaries, basic doctrine and Christian living.

### CHRISTIAN
## HERITAGE

Books representing some of the best material from the rich heritage of the church.

## MENTOR

Books written at a level suitable for Bible College and seminary students, pastors, and other serious readers. The imprint includes commentaries, doctrinal studies, examination of current issues and church history.

## CF4•K

Children's books for quality Bible teaching and for all age groups: Sunday school curriculum, puzzle and activity books; personal and family devotional titles, biographies and inspirational stories – because you are never too young to know Jesus!

Christian Focus Publications Ltd,
Geanies House, Fearn, Ross-shire,
IV20 1TW, Scotland, United Kingdom.
www.christianfocus.com
blog.christianfocus.com